FLIGHT

THE EVOLUTION OF AVIATION

Memorabilia captions, clockwise from top left:
- A lithograph poster by Ernest Montaut advertising the Grande Semaine d'Aviation de la Champagne which was held in August 1909 (p.30).
- The $25,000 Raymond Orteig prize won by Charles Lindbergh for the first non-stop flight from Paris to New York in 1927 (p.67).
- Congratulatory message from Louis Blériot to Amy Johnson after she became the first woman to fly solo from Britain to Australia in May 1930 (p.65).
- The British Airways Concorde fact sheet provided by the airline to passengers (pp.136–7).
- Front cover of newspaper Le Matin celebrating Blériot's Channel flight in 1909 (p.24).
- An Imperial Airways brochure promoting the boat/train services of the French shipping line Messageries Maritimes (p.61).
- A publicity leaflet produced by BOAC advertising their London–New York luxury "Monarch" passenger service (pp.112–3).
- A 1930s Imperial Airways air freight brochure (p.60).

THIS IS AN ANDRÉ DEUTSCH BOOK

This edition published in 2015 by André Deutsch
A division of the Carlton Publishing Group
20 Mortimer Street
London
W1T 3JW

First published in 2010

Design © Carlton Books Limited 2009, 2015
Text © Stephen Woolford and Carl Warner 2009

Printed in China

A CIP catalogue for this book is available from the British Library

ISBN: 978 0 23300 459 4

FLIGHT

THE EVOLUTION OF AVIATION

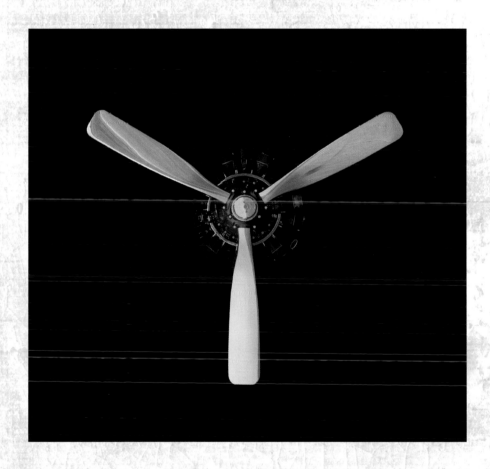

STEPHEN WOOLFORD &
CARL WARNER

ANDRE
DEUTSCH

CONTENTS

INTRODUCTION 6

TAKING FLIGHT 8

THE WRIGHT BROTHERS 14

LOUIS BLÉRIOT 20

THE BELLE EPOQUE 26

THE AEROPLANE GOES TO WAR 32

AIR FIGHTING 36

BOMBERS AND BOMBING 42

INDUSTRY AIRCRAFT AND AIR FORCES 46

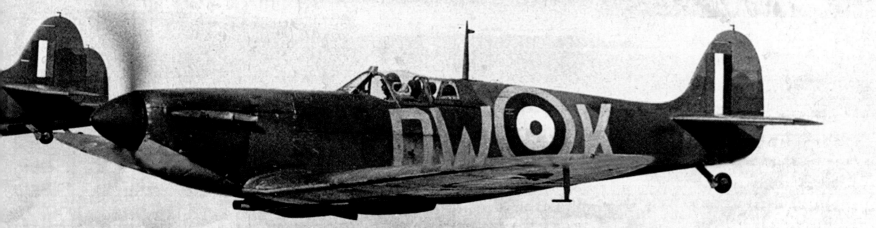

THE FIRST TRANSATLANTIC FLIGHTS 50

AVIATION IN THE 1920S AND 1930S 56

NEW YORK TO PARIS NON-STOP 62

AIRSHIP AND FLYING BOATS 68

THE FIRST MODERN AIRLINERS 72

THE APPROACH AND OUTBREAK
OF THE SECOND WORLD WAR 76

THE BATTLE OF BRITAIN & THE BLITZ 80

THE BOMBER WAR 86

WORKING WITH THE ARMIES 90

THE AIR WAR AT SEA 96

INDUSTRY AND NEW TECHNOLOGIES 102

AIR TRAVEL IN THE POST WAR WORLD 108

COLD WAR CONFRONTATION 114

AIR POWER IN KOREA AND VIETNAM 120

THE SPACE RACE 126

THE JET AGE 132

MODERN AIR POWER 138

AVIATION FOR ALL? 144

AVIATION AND THE MODERN WORLD 150

INDEX 156

TRANSLATIONS/CREDITS 158

INTRODUCTION

Manned heavier-than-air flight was undoubtedly one of the most important achievements of the twentieth century. It had a dramatic impact on many developments which we now regard as playing a crucial role in shaping the modern world.

As a tool for travel, the aircraft has brought people together. As a tool of war, it has all too frequently torn them apart. The aeroplane is one of the most recognisable symbols of modernity and technological innovation and aviation has become a huge industry, backed by vast technical and financial investment. But as we move forward into the twenty-first century the future of aviation, in an increasingly environmentally aware world, may be far less certain.

The story of flight is a global one. From Kitty Hawk, North Carolina, the site of the first flights by the Wright brothers, through to modern day Afghanistan and Iraq where aircraft have been at the forefront of conflict, our journey takes us across every continent of the world, into the skies above deserts and oceans and beyond, in times of peace and war. As much about people as it is about technology, it's a story of passengers and pilots, entrepreneurs and adventurers, scientists, soldiers, and astronauts, involving episodes of both high drama and terrible human tragedy.

Given the size and complexity of the subject, spanning as it does over one hundred years of outstanding endeavour, it is inevitable that this book could only ever be a series of snapshots illuminating the most outstanding stages in the history of flight. The selection of subject matter has been very much our own and the decision as to what to include and what to omit has been a difficult one; the evolution of aviation has so many enthralling facets.

In some ways the evolution of flight is a narrative of painstaking investigation and meticulous scientific study. In others, it is a tale of extreme courage and dogged determination. Happily, it is also a story that has left much behind in the way of fascinating documentary evidence, examples of which are included in many of the spreads in this book.

Stephen Woolford and Carl Warner

ACKNOWLEDGMENTS
First and foremost we would like to thank Kim Woolford and Alexandra Murphy for their support, encouragement and patience throughout the project. We are indebted to Gemma Maclagan and the team at Carlton, particularly designers Russell Knowles and David Ball and picture researchers Steve Behan and Ben White, without whom this book would not have begun (or ended).

TAKING FLIGHT

Watching birds in flight, it is easy to understand how our ancestors became fascinated by the idea of flying. History is littered with stories of would-be fliers who jumped from towers with artificial wings strapped to their arms. Inevitably, the wing-flapping "bird man" would plummet to the ground with dire consequences. Ancient myths tell of flying machines even more fanciful but there was one device, the kite, which did take to the air. Created in ancient China, there are even accounts of people attempting to fly attached to kites.

But it was with balloons that the first successful human flights were made. On 21 November 1783, Pilâtre de Rozier and the Marquis d'Arlandes made the first free flight, in a hot air balloon created by the Montgolfier Brothers. They flew from Paris for eight kilometres (five miles) at a height of 900 metres (3,000 feet). Work on hydrogen-filled balloons had been taking place in parallel with the Montgolfier's experiments, and on 1 December 1783, Jacques Charles and a companion lifted off from Paris for the first manned ascent in a hydrogen-filled balloon. The first balloon crossing of the English Channel was made only two years later by Jean-Pierre Blanchard and John Jeffries. Ballooning became a popular sport but practical uses were also found for balloons in nineteenth-century warfare, either to carry messages or as observation platforms. Balloons, however, have the drawback of being at the mercy of the winds. Powered and controlled airships do not have

ABOVE RIGHT A fourteenth-century manuscript showing a windsock kite carrying a bomb. Kites were introduced into Europe from China in the thirteenth century.

RIGHT Otto Lilienthal making a flight in 1894 in a monoplane hang glider. Lilienthal controlled his gliders by the dangerous practise of shifting the position of his body to maintain stability.

OPPOSITE Pilâtre de Rozier and the Marquis d'Arlandes made the first manned flight when they ascended over Paris in a Montgolfier hot air balloon on 21 November 1783. Ballooning developed in parallel, and often ahead of, heavier-than-air flight.

Dessiné par le Ch.^r de Lorimier.　　　　　　　　　　　　　　　Gravé par N. De Launay.

Premier Voyage Aërien　　　　　En présence de Mgr le Dauphin,
Experience faite　　　　　　　　　dans le Jardin de la Muette,
Sous la Direction　　　　　　　　de Mr Montgolfier,
Par M.^r le Marquis d'Arlandes　　et M. Pilatre du Rosier, le 21. 9.bre 1783.

Vüe de la Terrasse de Mr Franklin à Passi.

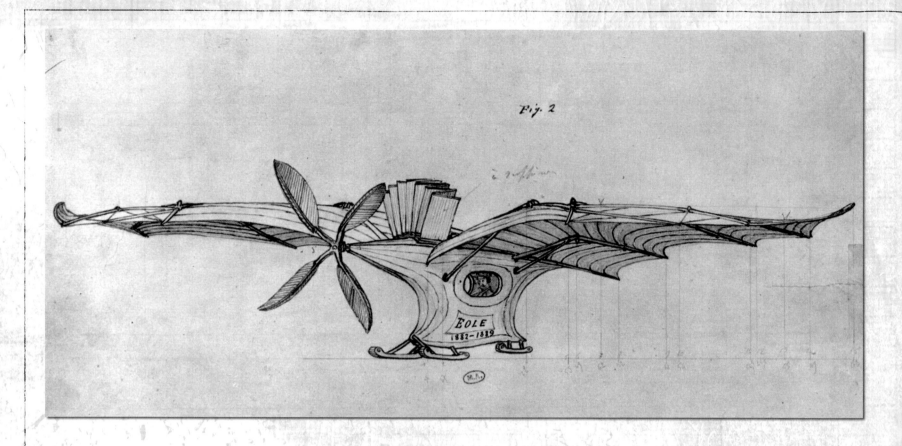

this disadvantage. In 1852, Frenchman Henri Giffard's airship used a small steam engine to drive a propeller mounted under a cigar-shaped balloon to fly 27 kilometres (17 miles).

Englishman George Cayley was the first to make real theoretical and practical progress towards heavier-than-air flight. In his experiments, he investigated the lift and drag created by different wings at various speeds and angles. Cayley applied what he had learnt to a series of glider models. This work culminated in his 1853 glider in which his coachman made a flight of 450 metres (1,500 feet) across Brompton Dale in Yorkshire. Cayley's work influenced aerial pioneers for the next 50 years.

Some of the early pioneers who followed on from Cayley tried to build powered flying machines; others had more success with

The Montgolfier Brothers

In 1782 Joseph-Michael (1740–1810) and Étienne (1745–1799) Montgolfier experimented with hot-air-filled silk bags which rose up because the heated air in the bags was lighter than the external air. However, the brothers did not realize this, believing that gas created by burning material caused the bags to rise. Nevertheless, in June 1783, their first public demonstration of a hot air balloon, consisting of an 11-metre (38-feet) paper-lined linen bag, was a success. In September of that year, at a royal demonstration at Versailles, a balloon was flown with a sheep, a rooster and a duck as its passengers. All returned safely to the ground. The first manned flight was made in November 1783.

OPPOSITE A drawing of Clément Ader's steam-powered *Éole*. Although not a practical and controllable flying machine, the *Éole* very briefly left the ground under its own power in 1890. Ader's next machine, the *Avion III*, failed to fly at all when tested in 1897.

BELOW Lilienthal in 1896 in Stölln near Berlin. Lilienthal crashed and died in the same year while flying a glider.

George Cayley
(1773–1857)

Sir George Cayley is sometimes referred to as "the father of aviation". He was an engineer and a Member of Parliament. He worked on a wide range of engineering projects but is best remembered for his pioneering work in aviation, developing the first proper understanding of the principles of flight. Cayley's 1804 model glider was similar in configuration to modern aircraft with monoplane wings towards the front and a tailplane with horizontal stabilizers and a vertical fin at the rear. His man-carrying glider first flew in 1853.

LEFT Sir George Cayley, "the father of aviation".

OPPOSITE Sir George Cayley's notes and sketches of the glider experiments he made in the summer of 1849.

gliders. In 1890, French engineer Clement Ader claimed that his steam-powered *Éole* had flown. It managed 50 metres (165 feet) at a height of 20 centimetres (eight inches). Then in 1894, in England, Hiram Maxim tested a steam-powered biplane on rails which lifted briefly. Neither Maxim, Ader or other exponents of the power-centred approach to aeroplane development, including the American Samuel Pierpont Langley, fully considered how they might control their aircraft if they actually flew, unlike experimenters who concentrated on gliding. Chief among these was the German Otto Lilienthal who developed his flying skills as he tested a series of 18 gliders in more than 2,000 flights, some of which were over 300 metres (1,000 feet), until his death during a crash landing in 1896.

Lilienthal influenced the work of American engineer and gliding experimenter Octave Chanute, who would in turn become a friend and mentor to the Wright brothers. It was to be the Wrights who successfully moved from gliding to the first controlled powered flight.

Brompton august the 30 1849 — I tried some experiments with a view to ascertain with accuracy the real angle that any plane makes with its line of flight when supporting a given weight & also the power shewn to be necessary in that line of flight to sustain that weight — the surface used was 16 28 feet of cotton cloth tightly stretched by two rods like those of a ship's sail, made flat to give little resistance to the air —

A strong pole 14½ feet long was the basis of this machine the two upright pieces kept these rods 10½ inches above the pole & put the center of gravity below the center of support & this center of gravity was 5 inches forwarder than the center of support & 10½ inches below it (say 5 inches) the whole machine weighed 16 pounds exactly — the sail contained 2½ square feet & was slightly elevated (about an angle of 8°) it had also a rudder to steer it towards either side containing say 1½ foot

The velocity varied in some of the flights but the least average was at the rate of 200 feet in 6 seconds the angle varied between 190 & 210 in the six seconds —

Hence a velocity of about 33 feet at an angle of 7° with the line of sail (or a 8th of a radius) sustains on 16 feet 16 pounds this agrees precisely with the weight of the cross & this surface of wing

THE WRIGHT
BROTHERS

Wilbur and Orville Wright had been interested in the problems associated with mechanical and human flight since childhood. They eagerly followed the fortunes of pioneers such as Otto Lilienthal, and in 1899 began to study the subject in depth. They requested all of the information then available on the subject from the Smithsonian, a US institution already deeply involved with aviation experiments, and identified the areas that needed further investigation.

They initially focused on "control", surmising that sustained flight would be achieved if adjustments could be continually made to the balance of a craft in order to keep it stable. To achieve this, Wilbur and Orville developed the idea of "wing warping"; twisting the flying surface to alter the flow of air and thus change the direction of the machine.

By September 1900, the Wrights had perfected the first of their experimental gliders and chosen Kitty Hawk, North Carolina, as a suitable location for trials. The glider was a success and the all-important wing warping control system worked well. But it did not generate as much lift as they had hoped. Further trials on a new glider, with redeveloped wings based on the work of earlier aviators, were even more disappointing. The brothers began to suspect that the calculations of earlier pioneers were crucially defective.

Wilbur and Orville commenced their own experiments, which ultimately completely

RIGHT The first flight photograph by John Daniels of Kill Devil HIlls lifesaving station, 17 December 1903.

The Wright Brothers

Wilbur (1867–1912) and Orville (1871–1948) were the sons of Milton and Susan Wright. Neither attended university, instead running several businesses, including the Wright Cycle Co. The profits from this successful enterprise were ploughed into their aviation experiments. In approach they were both meticulous and systematic. They matched their practical engineering skills with the ability to solve complex theoretical and scientific problems. The brothers combined this bookish intelligence with real passion for their work and the cool physical courage needed to test-fly their designs.

LEFT Orville and Wilbur Wright in their home town of Dayton, Ohio in 1909. Although the brothers were close from childhood, they often argued fiercely about the details of their work and challenged each other's point of view. This helped them to develop their ideas and turn them into practical working machines.

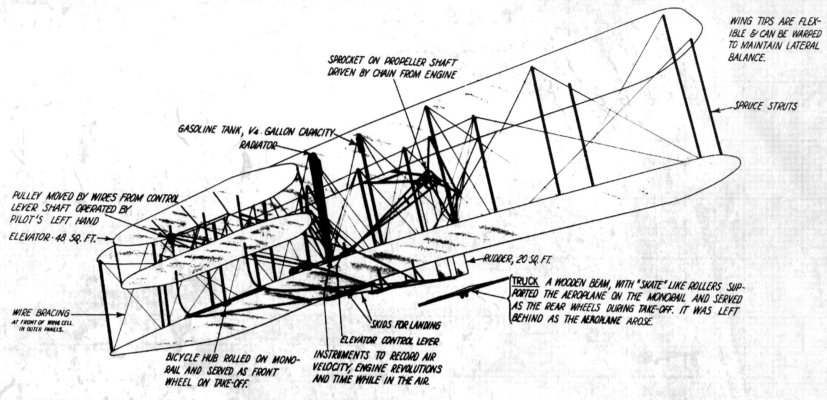

WING TIPS ARE FLEXIBLE & CAN BE WARPED TO MAINTAIN LATERAL BALANCE.

SPROCKET ON PROPELLER SHAFT DRIVEN BY CHAIN FROM ENGINE

SPRUCE STRUTS

GASOLINE TANK, 1/4 GALLON CAPACITY.

RADIATOR

PULLEY MOVED BY WIRES FROM CONTROL LEVER SHAFT OPERATED BY PILOT'S LEFT HAND

ELEVATOR · 48 SQ. FT.

RUDDER, 20 SQ. FT.

TRUCK A WOODEN BEAM, WITH "SKATE" LIKE ROLLERS SUPPORTED THE AEROPLANE ON THE MONORAIL AND SERVED AS THE REAR WHEELS DURING TAKE-OFF. IT WAS LEFT BEHIND AS THE AEROPLANE AROSE.

WIRE BRACING AT FRONT OF WING CELL IN OUTER PANELS.

SKIDS FOR LANDING

ELEVATOR CONTROL LEVER.

BICYCLE HUB ROLLED ON MONORAIL AND SERVED AS FRONT WHEEL ON TAKE-OFF.

INSTRUMENTS TO RECORD AIR VELOCITY, ENGINE REVOLUTIONS AND TIME WHILE IN THE AIR.

WING SPAN, 40 FT. 4 IN. – CHORD, 6 FT. 6 IN.
OVERALL LENGTH, 21 FT. 3/8 IN. – HEIGHT, 9 FT. 3 5/32 IN.
WING DROOP (ANTI-DIHEDRAL), 10 INCHES
WEIGHT, 605 POUNDS (WITHOUT PILOT).
WING AREA, 510 SQ. FT. – AIR SPEED, 31 MILES PER HOUR
WING LOADING, 1.46 LB. PER SQ. FT.
POWER LOADING, 62½ LB. PER HORSE POWER (WITH PILOT)
REVOLUTIONS PER MIN: ENGINE, 1025; PROPELLERS 356
(REDUCTION, ABOUT 3 TO 1)

PILOT LAY PRONE WITH HEAD FORWARD, HIS LEFT HAND OPERATING THE ELEVATOR LEVER, HIS HIPS IN A SADDLE. SHIFTING THE HIPS SIDEWISE PULLED WIRES ATTACHED TO THE SADDLE BY WHICH THE WING TIPS WERE WARPED AND THE RUDDER TURNED (A DOUBLE ACTION FROM ONE MOVEMENT) THUS CONTROLLING BALANCE AND DIRECTIONAL STEERING.

ABOVE The 1903 Wright Flyer. This aircraft made the world's first sustained, powered and controlled flight.

ABOVE The front page from the appropriately named *Virginian-Pilot* newspaper of 18 December 1903 records the achievement of the Wright brothers the day before at Kitty Hawk.

LEFT A granite monument to the Wright Brothers stands at Kill Devil Hills, North Carolina. The inscription reads "In commemoration of the conquest of the air by the brothers Wilbur and Orville Wright. Conceived by genius. Achieved by dauntless resolution and unconquerable faith".

Samuel P Langley
(1834–1906)

Samuel Pierpont Langley was one of the Wrights' most distinguished competitors. He was a gifted scientist and astronomer, who had gained a significant reputation in these fields before turning his attention to the problem of manned flight. He became Secretary of the Smithsonian Institution in 1887, which coincided with his increasing interest in aviation. First, he experimented with rubber-band, then steam-powered models. Then, using the resources of the Smithsonian, he progressed to build his famous *Acrodrome*. Langley's approach was the opposite of the Wrights'. He believed that given enough power, as long as the machine was inherently stable, it would fly. The result of this conviction was disappointment for Langley and Charles Manly, the engineer who had invented the powerplant for the *Aerodrome* and was chosen to test-fly it. During its December 1903 flight, Langley's massive machine was a failure. Days later, the Wrights' contrasting approach was triumphantly vindicated.

reworked those calculations. By mounting miniature experimental wing shapes on the front of a bicycle and then by using a specially-built wind-tunnel, the Wrights produced extremely accurate measurements that they then applied to their wing designs. In 1902, they tested a glider built using the data they had produced. When they added moveable vertical fins to the design, linked to the wing warping system, they soon began to glide for distances of up to 200 metres (656 feet). Control had been mastered.

The brothers then turned their attention to "power". They needed a light yet powerful engine, and none of the existing models were good enough. The Wrights decided to produce their own, asking their assistant Charlie Taylor to help. The resulting motor was a triumph of efficient design, weighing 81.65 kilograms (180 pounds) and delivering 12 horsepower. Designing an efficient propeller proved more complicated; working out the mathematical and physical principles involved taxed the brothers' skills enormously, but it also demonstrated the strength and value of their partnership. As Orville wrote later, "Our minds became so obsessed with it that we could do little other work. We engaged in innumerable discussions, and often after an hour or so of heated argument, we would discover that we were as far from agreement as when we started, but that both had changed to the other's original position in the discussion."

Eventually, the Wrights overcame the propeller issue, and they returned to Kitty Hawk in September 1903, with all of the components seemingly in place. Their attention was now firmly fixed on achieving sustained flight. Events elsewhere added impetus to their work, as a fellow aviation experimenter, Samuel P Langley, was preparing to launch his *Aerodrome* for the first time.

On 17 December 1903, after several weeks of frustrating setbacks, the Wrights launched their Flyer four times, with the men of the Kill Devil Hills lifesaving station acting as witnesses. With Orville at the controls, the machine initially spent 12 seconds in the air and covered a distance of 36.6 metres (120 feet). Two further attempts produced flights of greater distance. Then at noon, Wilbur began the fourth trip. This time the Flyer flew for an astonishing 59 seconds, a distance of 259.7 metres (852 feet). These two very special men from Ohio had achieved what many thought was impossible. Others would soon follow in their footsteps, but the honour of being first was theirs.

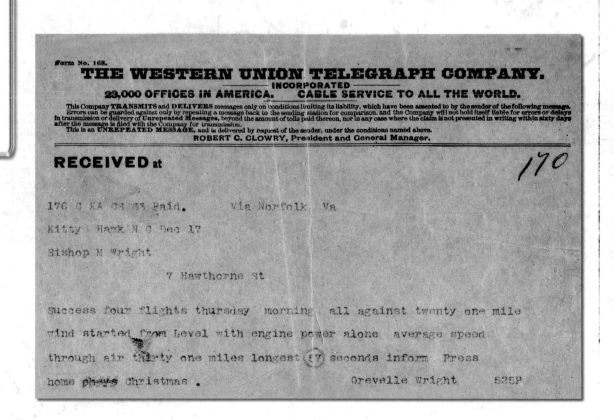

RIGHT A telegram from Orville Wright to his father Bishop Milton Wright, informing him of the brothers' successful flights on 17 December 1903.

Wilbur Wright
Orville Wright

Established in 1892

Wright Cycle Company

Van Cleve
Manufacturers of
Bicycles

1127 West Third Street

DAYTON, OHIO, Dec 28, 1903,

Dear Mr. Chanute,

Your telegram of congratulation
and the Christmas remembrances have reached us,
and, of course, we are deeply gratified at your
kindness.

The axles for which we were waiting
when you visited us, did not arrive for one whole
week after your departure. We spent part of
this time in installing a new system of operating
the wing tips and rear rudder, as the old system
did not seem quite satisfactory. We then spent
three days putting the axles in place again, and
giving the machine the final touches. When
ready for trial a three days storm kept us pen-
ned up so that another week was lost. We however made some indoor tests of the thrust of the propellers and found that we would have plenty of
power as the transmission only cost 5 or 10 percent
apparently, instead of the thirty percent you had
estimated. The thrust of the screw came within three
or four pounds of our calculation of what it would do
in a fixed position. But as we were concluding
these experiments a peculiar feeling led to an in-

Wright Cycle Company

1127 West Third Street

DAYTON, OHIO,

vestigation which revealed the fact that one of the axles was giving way. Accordingly we removed both of them and Orville went home to make new ones. He was gone two weeks more, so that by the time everything was ready again, five weeks had elapsed since the trouble with the axles began. We accordingly determined to try the machine at the earliest opportunity instead of waiting for the conditions we desired. So on the 14th inst although the wind was only 2 to 3 meters a second, thus making it necessary to use the hill in starting, we got the machine out and made the first trial. It rose from the track and soon reached a point as high as the starting point but as this was done too suddenly it lost speed somewhat so that it was no longer fully supported. In turning down to regain speed the rudder was moved too far, and the machine darted down and touched ground before it could be turned up again. The time was only 3½ seconds and the distance a little more than a hundred feet. The landing was made with the propellers still going, and with the machine sidling somewhat. The lower struts of the front rudder frame sunk into the sand and as it was braced only at the ends the

A letter dated 28 December 1903 from Wilbur Wright to fellow aviation pioneer Octave Chanute describing the Wright brothers' achievements earlier that month.

LOUIS BLÉRIOT
FIRST ENGLISH CHANNEL FLIGHT

Reports of the Wrights' achievements were treated with scepticism in Europe but pioneer aviators, particularly in France, were stirred into action by what they learnt of the brothers' aircraft. They were determined to do as well, if not better than the Americans, even though they were a long way behind. On 12 November 1906, Brazilian Alberto Santos-Dumont made the first powered heavier-than-air flight in Europe (220 metres/722 feet) at Bagatelle in Paris.

The following year, short flights were made by Louis Blériot and Robert Esnault-Pelterie in tractor (powered in front) biplanes. However real success came in 1908 with flights made in aircraft created by Gabriel Voisin and his younger brother Charles. These were biplanes with forward elevators and tails that looked like box kites but unlike the Wrights' Flyers, they lacked any means of lateral control. Despite this, Henri Farman won the *Grand Prix d'Aviation* by completing the first 1-kilometre- (three-fifths-of-a-mile-) circular flight in Europe on 13 January 1908 in a modified Voisin.

To protect their designs the Wrights had ceased flying in 1905, but pushed by the success of their rivals and with deals secured to sell their machines, they decided to take to the air again. Wilbur Wright went to France where, on 8 August 1908, he demonstrated the Flyer at Hunaudiers racetrack to an astonished crowd. His complete control over the aircraft prompted the French newspaper *Le Figaro* to report, "There is no doubt Wilbur and Orville Wright have well and truly flown …". Wilbur further demonstrated the practicability of the Wrights' aircraft with a series of flights ending in January 1909, spending a total of over 26 hours in the air, during which time he safely carried some 60 passengers. Among those who witnessed these flights was Louis Blériot. He realized that a new era in mechanical flight had commenced. Blériot, along with other French

Louis Blériot
(1872–1936)

Louis Blériot was an engineer and businessman who made his money manufacturing motor car lights. Blériot began to experiment with flying machines in 1900, developing his designs by trial and error, with Gabriel Voisin from 1903 to 1905 and on his own from 1906. His first success came in 1907 with the Blériot VII monoplane that he flew for 500 metres (1,650 feet). He moved on to the Blériot XI in which he made the world's first flight over a large body of water (50 kilometres/31 miles) when he crossed the English Channel in 37 minutes on 25 July 1909. The flight created a huge demand for the Blériot XI and Blériot's company was soon the largest aircraft manufacturer in the world. In 1914, Louis Blériot became the President of the SPAD company and turned it into one of France's leading manufacturers of combat aircraft. Blériot-Aeronautique switched to making commercial aircraft after the First World War.

ABOVE Hubert Latham made the first attempt to fly across the English Channel on 19 July 1909. He was forced to land on the sea when the engine of his Antoinette IV failed and was rescued by a French ship.

OPPOSITE Alberto Santos-Dumont made the first powered heavier-than-air flight in Europe to exceed 25m (82ft) on 23 October 1906 in his 14-bis, a box-kit type aircraft, at Bagatelle, Paris. In 1907 he created the Demoiselle monoplane, the precursor of the modern light plane.

Blériot XI monoplane

The Blériot XI was designed by Raymond Saulnier with input from Louis Blériot. With its front-mounted engine, tri-cycle undercarriage, front-mounted wings and rear-mounted tailplane, elevators and rudder, it established the basic aircraft shape still familiar to us today. The aircraft was powered by a 25-horsepower three-cylinder Anzani engine. Later versions had a 50-horsepower Gnome rotary engine. A weakness of early monoplanes was the stress placed on the externally braced wing. This led to them being replaced by biplanes. However some Blériot monoplanes were still flying at the start of the First World War.

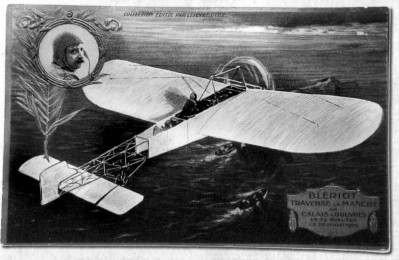

ABOVE An illustration commemorating Blériot's successful crossing of the English Channel on 25 July 1909. Helped by the publicity surrounding the flight, the Blériot XI became the main product of Louis Blériot's aircraft company before the First World War and the foundation of its commercial success.

aviation pioneers, was quick to incorporate wing warping; a key part of the Wrights' means of control, into his latest aircraft, the Blériot XI.

Impressed by the public's enthusiasm for the Wrights and keen to promote aviation as well as his newspaper sales, Lord Northcliffe, owner of the British *Daily Mail*, offered a "£1,000 prize for the first flight in a heavier-than-air machine across the Channel". In July 1909, the press converged on the French coast near

Calais, from where on a clear day, the white cliffs of Dover can be seen across the English Channel. Attention focused on two contenders for the prize, Louis Blériot in his Blériot XI and Hubert Latham. Latham made the first attempt in his Antoinette IV monoplane on 19 July. Unfortunately, its engine failed and Latham had to be rescued from the Channel by a French ship. After a period of bad weather, Blériot, who was suffering from a burnt foot from a previous flight, courageously decided to make

BELOW Louis Blériot and his wife Alicia pose for the press in front of Blériot's aircraft near Dover Castle, the day after the cross Channel flight in July 1909.

Vingt-Sixième Année. — N° 9281

ABONNEMENTS ANNONCES
SEINE & SEINE-&-OISE
ÉTRANGER

Stéphane LAUZANNE, Rédacteur en chef

Lundi 26 Juillet 1909

AGENCES A L'ÉTRANGER

Adresse Télégraphique : MATIN-PARIS
TÉLÉPHONE
103.04 — 103.05 — 103.06

Jules MADELINE, Président

Le Matin

SEUL JOURNAL FRANÇAIS RELIANT PAR SES FILS SPÉCIAUX LES QUATRE PREMIÈRES CAPITALES DU GLOBE

Un grand Français, Blériot, franchit la Manche en aéroplane

UNE DATE HUMAINE

CINQ HEURES DU MATIN. — Un coup de téléphone de Calais au « Matin » : « Blériot est parti à cinq heures moins vingt. »

CINQ HEURES ET DEMIE. — Un coup de téléphone de Douvres : « Blériot est arrivé. Un rédacteur du « Matin », agitant un drapeau français, lui a fait le signal d'atterrissement. »

Comme la vie est belle, en de pareils moments ! On sent que tout à coup l'homme vient de grandir et que, quoi que l'avenir vous réserve, on gardera jusqu'à sa mort la joie, parce qu'on a assisté, le dimanche 25 juillet 1909, à l'une des plus grandes fêtes de la science et de l'histoire, et que cette fête était donnée par la France.

Comment j'ai traversé la Manche

par Louis Blériot

Douvres, 25 Juillet.

Comment j'ai traversé la Manche ? Le fait est si simple que je renoncerais presque à le décrire, si, étant aviateur ce matin, je n'étais journaliste cet après-midi.

Le réveil fut pour moi quelque chose d'insupportable. Mon ami Alfred Leblanc, l'homme dévoué par excellence, m'avait réveillé à deux heures et demie. De n'étais, je l'avoue, nullement disposé à partir. Je voyais les choses en noir et — ne le dites à personne — j'aurais été heureux d'entendre dire que le vent soufflait si fort qu'aucune tentative n'était possible.

Enfin, cela n'allait pas du tout. Leblanc me remonta un peu. Il m'emporta dans son auto. J'étais sauvé. L'air vif qui me fouetta le visage me réveilla tout à fait. J'eus un peu honte de mon mouvement de faiblesse. J'avais cette fois du courage pour deux.

Aux Baraques, Mamet et Colin, mes deux excellents collaborateurs, ont ouvert la tente. Le monoplan sort de la tente, tiré par la ferme. Malgré l'heure matinale, le village est debout et de minute en minute des autos arrivent. Il y a bientôt quelques milliers de personnes. Cela me gêne un peu. J'aurais si bien voulu être seul.

Nous décidons, Leblanc et moi, qu'un essai préliminaire va avoir lieu. On range la foule tant bien que mal. L'appareil s'élève aisément. Ce calme, la surcharge du cylindre d'air m'en diminue que faiblement la puissance. J'ai une hélice nouvelle qui tire dans la perfection. Je reste une dizaine de minutes dans les airs, agréablement surpris de constater sur un petit vent frais qui vient de la terre, un vent de marée qui me poussera vers la Manche.

*   *
*

Tout est prêt. Fidèle au règlement, j'ai attendu le lever du soleil. Leblanc m'indique que le disque est apparu au moyen d'un fanion qu'il agite sur la dune. C'est le signal. Une certaine émotion s'empare de moi au moment où je prends place dans l'appareil. Que va-t-il arriver ? Irai-je jusqu'à Douvres ? Ah ! diable ! où suis-je donc ?

Je me dirige droit devant moi, m'élève progressivement de mètre en mètre ; je franchis la dune d'où Leblanc m'envoie ses souhaits. Je suis à présent au-dessus de la mer, laissant à ma droite le « contre-torpilleur qui m'attend. Une fumée opaque obscurcit le soleil. Dieu ! il est tout à coup on allait m'objecter que Phébus n'est pas au premier tiers de sa route ?

Je vais, je vais tranquillement, sans aucune émotion, sans aucune impression réelle. Il me semble être en ballon. L'absence de tout vent me permet de ne faire agir aucune commande du gouvernail ou du gauchissement. Si je pouvais bloquer ces commandes, je pourrais mettre les deux mains dans les poches. Ah ! le brave garçon !

Je veux atterrir ; le remous est violent. Dès que j'approche du sol, un tourbillon de vent me prend. Je me précipite pourtant. Est-il parti ? Serait-il tombé ?

*   *
*

Bientôt je perçois un bruit vague, puis un ronflement étrange. A ce moment, je

his attempt early in the morning of 25 July. He soon overtook a French destroyer escort and after ten minutes realized that as he checked his direction, he could not see the ship, France or England. Pressing on, Blériot glimpsed the English coast, headed for it and, caught by a gust of wind, made a crash landing in a field above the cliffs at Dover. Uninjured, Blériot's place in history was assured. He had made the world's first flight over a large body of water, some 36.5 kilometres (23.5 miles), which he crossed in 37 minutes. But for the British there was the realization that the Channel no longer gave them the same security that they had previously enjoyed.

ABOVE Louis Blériot acknowledges the applause of crowds in London on 26 July 1909 while on his way to meet Lord Northcliffe to accept the prize for the first flight across the Channel. Blériot also received a hero's welcome on his return to Paris a few days later.

OPPOSITE Front cover of newspaper *Le Matin* celebrating Blériot's Channel flight, Monday 26 July 1909. The headline reads "A great Frenchman, Blériot, crosses the Channel in an aeroplane". It uses the French term for the Channel – La Manche, meaning "sleeve".

RIGHT Postcard produced after Blériot's flight, it reads "I'm going to London by air so I won't be sea-sick".

THE BELLE
EPOQUE

The world's first major aviation meeting, the *Grande Semaine d'Aviation de la Champagne*, was held in France near Reims between 22 and 29 August 1909. It attracted a crowd of nearly 200,000 spectators and firmly established aviation as a viable technology. Interest focused on three competitions, distance, speed and altitude. The distance competition was won by Henri Farman who flew a record 180 kilometres (112 miles). The prize for highest speed over a distance of 30 kilometres (19 miles) was won by American Glen Curtiss at an average speed of 75 kilometres per hour (47 miles per hour). Louis Blériot was a close second. Hubert Latham won the altitude contest by flying to an unprecedented 155 metres (508 feet).

Reims set the pattern for the many air meetings that followed across Europe and the United States. Undoubtedly crashes were part of the attraction of these spectacles; 32 pilots, out of fewer than 600 worldwide, were killed in 1910. Crowds also came to expect more complex and dangerous flying. French pilot Adolphe Pégoud was the first to include the "loop the loop" stunt in his display in 1913, a year in which the French also dominated record and distance flying. Roland Garros made the first non-stop flight across the Mediterranean from France to Tunisia, Marcel Prévost set a new speed record of 204 kilometres per hour (126.7 miles per hour) and Edmond Perreyon, Blériot's chief test pilot, reached an altitude of 6,120 metres (20,079 feet).

In the United States, development moved at a slower pace. The Wright Brothers' aircraft company was set up in 1909 at Dayton, Ohio

Glenn Curtiss
(1878–1930)

Glen Curtiss was a motorcycle manufacturer (he set a world motorcycle speed record of 219 kilometres per hour [136 miles per hour] in 1907) who moved into aviation after working with Alexander Graham Bell's Aerial Experiment Association. In 1908 their "June Bug" won the Scientific American Trophy for the first public flight in the US of more than one kilometre (0.6 miles). A Curtiss Model D made the first take-off from a ship in 1910. By 1914, Curtiss was the biggest aircraft manufacturer in the United States. The company produced 10,000 aircraft during the First World War, including the famous JN-4 trainer and flying boats.

ABOVE Spectators stand on chairs to get a better view of the aeroplanes during the *Grande Semaine d'Aviation de la Champagne*, near Reims, France in August 1909. The event was the precursor of many aviation meetings held in the years before the First World War.

OPPOSITE Alliot Verdon Roe test flies the Roe II Triplane, the first product of the newly formed A V Roe and Company, in 1910. Later known as Avro, the company went on to become a major British aircraft manufacturer. In 1909 Roe had been the first to make a flight in an all-British aeroplane.

and their aeroplanes were made under licence by European companies, including Britain's Short Brothers. But the Wrights soon ceased to be market leaders as they became entangled in legal actions for infringements of their patents. Foremost of these was the case against Glen Curtiss which went on until 1914. Curtiss was a successful motorcycle manufacturer who turned to aviation in 1907 and who by 1914 was the leading aircraft manufacturer in the US. Exhausted by the litigation, Wilbur Wright died of typhoid fever in 1912 and Orville sold his interest in the Wright Company in 1915.

There was a steady expansion of aircraft types from 1909. The first flight from water was made by Henri Fabre in his seaplane, *The Hydravia*, in March 1910. In 1912, Glen Curtiss achieved another first by designing a flying boat, an aircraft with a boat-like hull. In Germany, aviation was dominated by the creations of Count Ferdinand von Zeppelin.

ABOVE Pilot Harriet Quimby prepares to take off. In 1911 Quimby became the first licensed female pilot in the United States and in April of the following year, the first woman to fly across the English Channel. Only a few months later she died in a flying accident during a display at Boston Harbor in the US in July 1912.

BELOW Cyclists standing on their bicycles peer over the perimeter fence to watch the 1911 Hendon aviation meeting. Under the leadership of Claude Grahame-White, Hendon became a major centre for aviation activity in Britain and after the First World War was best known for its annual RAF air displays.

Voisin Brothers

Gabriel Voisin (1880–1973) trained as an industrial designer. In 1900 he was hired as a designer for the Universal Exposition in Paris where he met Clément Ader, who sparked off his interest in aviation. He started experimenting with a glider in 1903–1904 and in 1905 began working with Louis Blériot. Their partnership ended in late 1906 and Gabriel and his brother Charles (1882–1912), then established *Les Frères Voisin*, one of the world's first aeroplane factories, at Billancourt, Paris. Their 1907 Voisin was used by many leading aviators, including Henri Farman. The company went on to produce over 10,000 aircraft by 1918.

ABOVE The Sopwith Tabloid in which Briton Harold Pixton won the Schneider Trophy, a speed race for seaplanes, in April 1914 at Monaco, France. Pixton flew at an average speed of 139.4 kilometres per hour (86.6 miles per hour).

OPPOSITE A lithograph poster by Ernest Montaut advertising the *Grande Semaine d'Aviation de la Champagne* which was held near Reims in August 1909. The event was sponsored by local champagne producers.

His airships were large, steerable, powered, lighter-than-air, craft consisting of a rigid framework containing gas bags filled with hydrogen to provide lift. By 1914 and the start of the First World War, Zeppelins had carried 37,000 passengers aloft. One flight, more than any other, demonstrated the potential of the aircraft. On 30 June 1914, pilot and designer Igor Sikorsky and three crew took off from St Petersburg in his large four-engined *Il'ya Muromets* for a successful 2,600-kilometre- (1,600-mile-) flight to Kiev and back. Sikorsky's design was adapted as a long-range bomber during the First World War, as were Zeppelin's airships.

The internationally tense years before 1914 saw the military take an increasing interest

in the aeroplane. The French formed the Aéronautique Militaire in 1910 and the Imperial German Army Air Service was formed in the same year. The Russian Army Air Service was established in 1912 as was the British Royal Flying Corps (RFC). Initially, the RFC had a military and a naval wing but the separate Royal Naval Air Service (RNAS) was formed in 1914. The RFC and the RNAS subsequently joined together in 1918 to form the Royal Air Force (RAF). As the world slid towards war, the nascent pioneer aircraft companies such as Voisin, Farman, Blériot, Breguet and Nieuport in France, Albatros, Rumpler, Aviatik and Fokker in Germany and Avro, Handley Page Sopwith and Bristol in Britain – plus many more – began to expand and switch to large scale production.

THE AEROPLANE
GOES TO WAR

Military aviation was in its infancy when the European powers went to war in August 1914 at the start of what we now know as the First World War. However, by the end of the war in 1918, the air had joined the land and the sea as a place in which men fought and died, and from which attacks were launched on both military and civilian targets.

At the start of the war, the main combatant nations – Britain, France and Russia on the one side and Germany and Austro-Hungary on the other – could muster fewer than 500 serviceable aircraft for military or naval purposes. The military had one main use for these simple, initially unarmed and often unreliable biplanes and monoplanes – reconnaissance; finding out what the other side was doing. In this, aeroplanes were seen as an adjunct to the cavalry, the army's traditional scouting force, but as the conflict developed they soon came to replace it and make a significant contribution of their own to the conduct of the war.

Royal Aircraft Factory
BE2c

The BE2 was designed before the war in 1912 at the Royal Aircraft Factory by Geoffrey de Havilland. It first flew in 1912, and at the time it out-performed its competitors, but by 1914 it was recognized that this unarmed and slow aircraft needed upgrading. The improved BE2c was very stable and this made the aircraft good for aerial reconnaissance work, but its slow speed and ineffective armament made it an easy target for enemy fighters. Industry was geared up to produce the BE2c in large numbers so it stayed in production far longer than it should have.

ABOVE The BE2c was the first armed version of the Royal Aircraft Factory's BE2 reconnaissance aircraft. The machine gun was carried in the forward cockpit, greatly restricting the observer's field of fire.

RIGHT A German balloon being manoeuvred into position. Both sides used tethered balloons as observation platforms. Balloons were not easy to attack from the air as they were heavily defended by batteries of guns on the ground but in case they were hit, the observers were equipped with parachutes. Aircraft pilots were not issued with parachutes until 1918, when German crews became the first to use them.

Geoffrey de Havilland
(1882–1965)

Geoffrey de Havilland was one of aviation's great design and manufacturing pioneers. He joined what was to become the Royal Aircraft Factory in 1910 and moved to the Aircraft Manufacturing Company (Airco) in 1914 to become its chief designer. Aircraft designed by de Havilland accounted for over 30 per cent of Allied aircraft and some 95 per cent of American wartime production. He set up the de Havilland Aircraft Company in 1920. Among its many products was the Moth series of light aeroplanes, the fast and versatile Second World War Mosquito and the Comet, the first jet airliner.

As the Germans advanced in Western Europe, the Allied armies were forced to retreat, but information gathered by aircraft helped them to halt the advance and launch counter-attacks that forced the invaders back. This war of movement ended when neither side could get around the other and both were forced to dig defensive trench lines that by the winter of 1914–1915 stretched from the English Channel to the Swiss border. For the next three-and-a half-years, as millions of soldiers became locked in the bitter relentless struggle of trench warfare, only observers in aeroplanes and tethered balloons could effectively see and record what was happening along and across the Western Front.

Reconnaissance aircraft such as the BE2c were generally two-seaters carrying a pilot and an observer. While the pilot concentrated on flying the aircraft, the observer gathered information. Initially this was recorded by

sketches, but from 1915 photography became the principal aerial reconnaissance technique. Whole sections of the trenches could be photographed in detail. These photographs were then joined together to form large "photo mosaics" which could be interpreted for essential information or intelligence that was used both to determine the enemy's intentions and to plan attacks against them.

A related task for aircraft and their crews was artillery spotting. Massive artillery barrages fired against defensive positions both preceded and continued throughout offensives. They never achieved a decisive effect, however, until the return to more mobile warfare during 1918, the last year of the war, when they were used in conjunction with other means of assault, including low flying, strafing and bombing aircraft. Aircraft observers could spot where artillery shells fell and with the introduction of effective wireless transmitters

from 1915, could communicate target co-ordinates by Morse code to the gunners who then directed their fire accordingly.

Intelligence gathered through photo-reconnaissance had to be frequently updated so patrols were flown every day alongside regular artillery-spotting flights. Initially, the main threats faced by the aircraft crews came from the weather, fire from the ground, and the unreliability of their machines, but as they started to arm themselves; first of all with rifles or hand-thrown bombs and then machine-guns, the war in the air became far more dangerous. In 1914, the Allies probably held the upper hand but with the introduction of purpose-built fighter aircraft in 1915, the reconnaissance aircraft suffered as they flew on their steady patrol lines. Forty seven of the 80 aircraft destroyed by the German ace Manfred von Richthofen were engaged on reconnaissance duties!

OPPOSITE French cavalry watch an aeroplane passing overhead in 1914. Aircraft came to replace cavalry in its traditional role of scouting for the armies.

AIR FIGHTING
IN THE FIRST WORLD WAR

Fighter aircraft were developed to prevent or disrupt the work of reconnaissance and artillery-spotting aeroplanes over the Western Front. After 1915, they were generally single-seat aircraft armed with a machine-gun, or guns, that were aimed by pointing the fighter at the target. Once fighters began to appear in large numbers in 1916, each side attempted to stop the other from destroying their reconnaissance aircraft. This led to fighter combats and an ongoing battle to control the skies over the battlefields.

ABOVE Successful pre-war aviator Roland Garros in June 1911. Garros joined the French air service at the outbreak of war and in April 1915 achieved the first-ever shooting-down of an aircraft in which a machine gun was fired through a propeller fitted with deflector plates. He shot down two more enemy aircraft before he too went down and both he and his aircraft were captured by the Germans.

RIGHT A British Sopwith F 1 Camel. The Camel destroyed more German aircraft than any other Allied aircraft during the First World War. It could be difficult to fly but in the hands of a competent pilot the Camel proved a very manoeuvrable fighter.

Arming a fighter aircraft with a machine gun was not easy. The weapon had to be light and accessible to the pilot and this meant that it had to be mounted either above the engine and fired through the arc of the propeller or above the top wing of a biplane. The former was problematic as the bullets could hit the propeller. The French tried placing metal plates on the propeller to deflect bullets should they hit the blades but this was unreliable and very dangerous. Another alternative was to use a pusher type aircraft, in which the engine and propeller were mounted behind the pilot, leaving the field of fire forward clear. The

Germans came up with the best solution when they fitted an interrupter mechanism to their Fokker Eindecker monoplane. This paused the machine gun when the propeller was in the line of fire. Using the Fokker, the Germans took control of the skies over their trenches during the winter of 1915–1916, shooting down so many Allied aircraft that British Royal Flying Corps (RFC) pilots referred to themselves as "Fokker Fodder".

In preparation for their offensive against the French at Verdun in February 1916, the Germans formed specialist units of fighters and developed air-fighting tactics that took

a growing toll on French machines. To regain the initiative, the French re-equipped their air units with the Nieuport Scout, whose gun was mounted on the aircraft's upper wing and concentrated their fighter squadrons into bigger groups. By May 1916, the German air service had lost the struggle for air supremacy over Verdun. The RFC also reorganized its squadrons and by June 1916 its fighter units, equipped with the de Havilland DH2, a pusher design, and Nieuport Scouts, gained the edge over the Germans during the Battle of the Somme. However, the Allied success was short-lived and the Germans hit back with new

ABOVE Captain Albert Ball seated in the cockpit of a Royal Aircraft factory SE5a. With at least 44 victories to his credit, Ball was killed in May 1917 while flying with No 56 Squadron, RFC.

LEFT Captain Edward V Rickenbacker of the United States air service. Rickenbacker scored 26 victories between April and November 1918 and was the leading American ace of the First World War.

Manfred von Richthofen
(1892–1918)

With 80 victories to his name, Baron Manfred von Richthofen was the top-scoring fighter pilot of the First World War. He died on 21 April 1918 flying a red Fokker DrI Triplane. The RAF credited this as an aerial victory to Canadian Captain Roy Brown but there is considerable evidence to suggest that Richthofen was in reality killed by ground fire. The baron was a fine leader of the JG1 mobile unit, the famous "Flying Circus", but showed few signs of chivalry in combat, ruthlessly hunting down his victims. Today he is still remembered in popular culture as the Red Baron after the red colour of the aircraft he flew.

AVIATION MILITAIRE

12ᵉ Groupe de Combat

(1)   ACTIVE

(2) AVIATION – ESCADRILLE N – 3 .

(1) Active, Réserve ou Territoriale
(2) Corps ou Service.
(3) Arme ou Service.
(4) Pour le Sous-Officier, la date de nomination au **grade de Sous-Officier.**

MÉMOIRE DE PROPOSITION

pour Citation à l'Ordre de l'Armée.

(3)   AVIATION

	MOTIF de la proposition et avis du **Chef de Corps** ou du Service

NOM   GUYNEMER

PRÉNOMS   GEORGES

Numéro matricule

Grade   Capitaine

Date d'entrée au service   21 Novembre 1914

Durée des services effectifs. . .   2 ans   8 mois   10 jours.

Durée des services dans la réserve (s'il y a lieu) . . . . . .   ans   mois   jours.

Date de nomination au grade actuel de la Légion d'Honneur . . . { CHEVALIER : 24 Décembre 1915 / OFFICIER : 11 Juin 1917.

Date de la nomination au grade actuel dans la hiérarchie (4) . . . { 21 Février 1917

Motif (manuscrit): Pilot de combat incomparable. Le 6 et 7 juillet a abattu ses 46ᵉ 47ᵉ et 48ᵉ avions ennemis.

Le 5 juillet, a livré un combat très dur, au cours duquel, il a été descendu pour la septième fois, son avion criblé de balles.

	ANS.	MOIS.	JOURS.
SERVICES : Active et Réserve	2	8	10
MAJORATIONS — Etudes préliminaires			
MAJORATIONS — Légion d'Honneur	1	7	8
MAJORATIONS — Séjour dans garnison frontière			
MAJORATIONS — Aviation			
MAJORATIONS — Etc			
Blessures	2		
Citations à l'Ordre de l'Armée	21		
Campagnes	2	8	10
TOTAUX	29	11	28

Blessures de Guerre 1 le 12 Mars (VERDUN) 1 le 23 Sep. 16 (SOMME)

Citations 21 à l'O/de l'Armée:21/7, 5/9, 12/12-15;9/2, 26/3, 25/5, 25/6, 27/7, 24/8, 28/8, 3 & 23/9, 28/10, 20 & 26/12-16;28/11/16

Actions d'éclat 12, 13 & 14/2, 26/3, 14/6, - 1917.

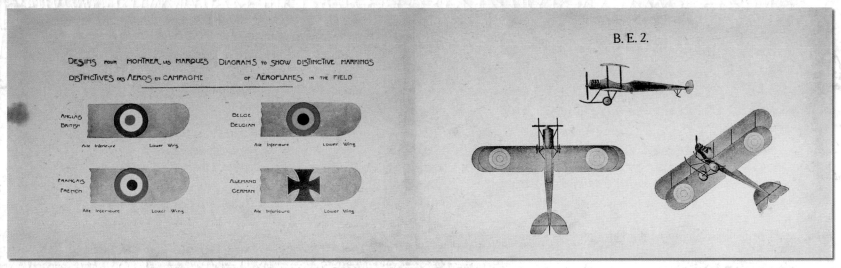

aircraft such as the Albatros DIII and grouped their squadrons into large mobile units, which could be deployed where needed to achieve local air superiority. The most famous of these was Jagdgeschwader 1 (JG1) led by Manfred von Richtofen. Its brightly coloured aircraft were known to the British as Richtofen's "Flying Circus". Such was the level of German success that during "Bloody April" 1917 the life expectancy of new RFC pilots was less than three weeks. New aircraft such as the Spad XIII, the SE5a and the Sopwith Camel swung the battle back in the Allies' favour in the summer of 1917. Despite the introduction of the excellent Fokker D VII in the following year, the German Air Service was overwhelmed by the mass of Allied aircraft deployed against it and by the end of the war in November 1918, could do little save mount local challenges to the Allies' dominance of the air.

Air combat gave rise to the phenomenon of the "ace", a status given to fliers who achieved a certain number of "kills" or victories (initially five, but the number increased as the war went on). These fliers became public heroes and were portrayed as "knights of the air", but air fighting was rarely chivalrous and was as deadly as that on the ground.

Georges Guynemer
(1894–1917)

Captain Guynemer was not the highest-scoring French ace, but this modest, frail man captured the French people's hearts. So much so that when he failed to return from a patrol on 11 September 1917, many could not accept he had been killed and preferred to think he had simply flown off into the clouds. Guynemer was credited with 53 victories. He flew some 660 hours and took part in more than 600 combats, mainly in Nieuports and Spads. Guynemer is still remembered in France today and a monument to him stands in front of the headquarters of the *Armée de l'Air in Paris.*

ABOVE A bi-lingual guide to aircraft recognition and insignia from the first half of the First World War.

OPPOSITE A note proposing a mention in Despatches for Captain Georges Guynemer following actions in July 1917 in which he scored his 46th, 47th and 48th victories.

BOMBERS
AND BOMBING

In 1914, the only aircraft capable of carrying a significant bomb load that also had the ability to reach strategic targets beyond the battlefield were the massive metal-framed Zeppelin and wooden-framed Schütte-Lanzes, airships of the Imperial German Navy and Army. In his 1908 novel *The War in the Air*, HG Wells described a fictional airship attack on New York. During the First World War, fiction turned to reality as German airships attacked French cities, including Paris, and in particular Britain, which was hit for the first time on 19 January 1915. Attacking at night, the German airships made a further 50 raids on Britain but their impact was limited as British defences improved. One of the most effective weapons used against them was explosive and incendiary ammunition fired from defending aircraft. The sight of a hydrogen-filled airship exploding was a horrendous spectacle not easily forgotten by any who witnessed it.

Of more consequence were raids on London and Paris by large German Gotha multi-engine bombers and the even larger R-planes. These started in May 1917 and in June of that year, London was hit by two dramatic daylight raids. Public outrage led to an immediate improvement in the city's defences. These became so effective that by September, the bombers had to attack by night. The raiders continued to get through, but as the air defence system, which included observer posts, anti-aircraft guns, searchlights, barrage balloons and fighters organized from control rooms, was improved, the Gothas suffered heavier losses. These, together with the German's need to use the bombers on the Western Front, led to the raids' ending in May 1918.

The raids did not affect the Allies ability to make war on Germany but they did force them to divert important resources to air defence that might otherwise have been used at the battlefront. Over 1,300 people were killed in Britain during the raids, a relatively small number compared with military casualties but one that made a deep impression on the British people, who demanded reprisal attacks on Germany.

The French made bombing raids on Germany from 1915 but inflicted little damage. Attacks by the British Royal Naval Air Service (RNAS) in late 1916 and 1917 were also unsuccessful. Following the raids on London, there was a fresh impetus to renew attacks on Germany and to reorganize Britain's air services, and in April

ABOVE After a German airship raid on London in 1915, soldiers and civilians gather in the streets between bomb-damaged buildings. London was bombed for the first time on 31 May that year.

LEFT "Londoners fear the Zeppelin" – a 1914 German propaganda card. Although the German airship attacks killed 557 people, their effect on the course of the war was limited and by 1916 British defence measures began to prevail.

OPPOSITE A British Handley Page 0/400 coming in to land. The 0/400 was the RAF's main long-range strategic bomber during the First World War but the war ended before the Allied bombing campaign against Germany could have much effect.

1918 the Royal Air Force (RAF) was formed. In June 1918, the RAF also established the Independent Air Force (IAF) in France under Major-General Trenchard. Its mission was to bomb Germany, but the majority of its operations were tactical in support of the Allied armies, which now included the Americans (who had entered the war in 1917). The conflict ended before the IAF could conduct a sustained strategic bombing campaign and its raids on Germany had little effect. However, if the war had continued, the campaign would have been stepped up with new aircraft such as the British Vickers Vimy and the French Farman Goliath.

Italy joined the Allies in 1915, and used its large Caproni bombers to attack Austria. Italian Giulio Douhet called for Italy to create a large bomber force but Italian raids, like those of its allies, were also limited in effect. Nevertheless, air power advocates such as Douhet, the American General Billy Mitchell, and Trenchard, had a profound effect on inter-war thinking about the threat and war-winning potential of the strategic bomber.

Handley Page 0/400

At the start of the war, the British Admiralty had responsibility for the defence of the United Kingdom against air attack. It had some success raiding German airship bases, but decided it needed larger aircraft. This led to the development of the Handley Page 0/100 which flew in 1915 and the improved 0/400 of 1918. This large (it had a 30-metre [100-foot] wing span) twin-engine bomber equipped squadrons of the RAF's Independent Air Force which carried out night raids on Germany. The four-engine Handley Page V/1500 went in to production in 1918 but was too late for its planned use of raiding Germany from bases in eastern England.

Peter Strasser
(1876–1918)

Peter Strasser was commander of the Imperial German Navy's airship fleet during the First World War. Under Strasser, airships attacked London, Paris, Antwerp and other ports and cities. Strasser strove to make the airship an effective weapon and believed that Britain could be beaten by the destruction of its cities, factories and dockyards. He regularly flew on missions, but was killed before he could achieve his ambition of a decisive raid across the Atlantic on New York. Strasser's Zeppelin L70 was shot down off the east coast of England on 5 August 1918. There were no survivors.

INDUSTRY
AIRCRAFT AND AIR FORCES

During the First World War the aeroplane developed into an effective and reliable machine used by the military for reconnaissance, artillery-spotting, air-fighting, ground-strafing, tactical and strategic bombing; roles that would continue throughout subsequent conflicts. Aircraft and airships were also used at sea by naval air services. Airships, particularly non-rigid airships, or blimps as they became known, together with flying boats, were used for long-range reconnaissance and increasingly important anti-submarine work.

The Royal Naval Air Service was quick to see the potential of deploying aeroplanes on ships. It first used seaplanes on carriers converted from cross-Channel ferries and then modified HMS *Furious* with a forward aircraft deck in August 1917. Taking off was comparatively easy, but landing was much more difficult. Squadron Commander E H Dunning managed this twice in a Sopwith Pup in August 1917 but was drowned on the third attempt. In 1918 HMS *Argus*, the first true aircraft carrier, proved more successful.

If the war had continued, the Navy would have used it to launch an attack on its German counterpart.

The aircraft available to the military in 1914 were produced mainly by small companies, but these grew into large industrial concerns supported by government backing and contracts. Companies from outside aviation, particularly motor-car manufactures, also became involved in the burgeoning aircraft industry, along with a host of engineering sub-contractors. The war became a battle

for production as well as a battle for control of the skies. It was a war that the Allies won convincingly. For example, Britain made 55,092 airframes during the conflict, whilst France made 51,700 and Germany just 38,000.

The Allies took a fairly con-servative approach to aircraft design and construction materials. Their aeroplanes were largely wooden-framed, fabric-covered biplanes strengthened with struts and wires. More powerful and reliable engines gave improved

LEFT With the help of crew members on the deck of HMS Furious on 2 August 1917, Squadron Commander E H Dunning in a Sopwith Pup, makes the first landing on a moving ship. Dunning died five days later trying to repeat his success.

RIGHT Aircraft manufacturer Anthony Fokker (centre) poses with German flying aces Bruno Loerzer (left) and Herman Göring (right) in 1918. Unable to make aircraft in Germany after the war, Fokker moved to the US and established a successful company there. Göring led the German air force during the Second World War and Loerzer served under him, commanding units during the Battle of Britain in 1940.

BELOW No. 1 Squadron RAF with their SE5a aircraft at Claremarais, France in 1918. At the end of the war in November 1918, the RAF was the world's largest air force, operating over 26,000 aircraft from 675 airfields.

I AM SHIP No. 1
WILL LEAVE FOR FRANCE
4 30 P.M.

performance. Killing power was increased with the addition of more machine-guns or by building bigger machines capable of carrying greater bomb loads over longer distances. The Germans were more creative in their use of materials. Welded steel tubing was used for frames and on some aircraft plywood was shaped to create the outer surface. They were also the first to introduce an all-metal aircraft, the Junkers J 4, an armoured infantry support monoplane made of duralumin which went into combat from 1917. The Junkers J 8 with its cantilevered wing (a wing with no external bracing) was even more innovative and indicated the direction aircraft design was to take.

By 1918, the era of the lone ace hunting his prey had passed. Air fighting had come to rely on teamwork and larger formations. Up to 60 aircraft at a time might be seen manoeuvring for position before attacking and breaking up into the whirling mass of a "dog-fight". Air forces also grew into complex organizations that deployed large numbers of men, women and machines. In 1918, with nearly 300,000 personnel the RAF was the largest. It was also the first air force to be organized separately and independently from an army or navy.

The creation of the long-range bomber was to give the air forces their main independent strategic mission. It was the arrival of these large aircraft that also led to the development of commercial aviation as well as the destruction of European and Japanese cities from the air in the Second World War.

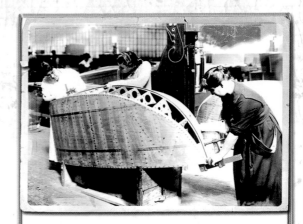

ABOVE Female factory workers construct the wing-tip of a naval aircraft, c.1918.

Aircraft Factories

Pre-war manufacturers re-used existing large open structures to make aircraft. During the war, these facilities were expanded and many new factories built. Aircraft were constructed in batches with the fuselages on trestles and then on their wheels so they could be moved efficiently through the factories. Wings and other sub-assemblies were added, then the aircraft were covered in fabric and the engine and other components installed. For the first time, thousands of women worked in the factories undertaking tasks previously carried out by men. However, many lost their jobs when the aircraft industry contracted after the war and the men returned to work.

LEFT The 1000th DH4 to be made at the Dayton-Wright Airplane Company in the US, photographed in July 1918. Entering the war in 1917 the US opted to build European combat designs under licence in order to save time and deliver aircraft to the front quickly.

Hugh Trenchard
(1873–1956)

Hugh Trenchard joined the British Army in 1893. He fought in the Boer War and later saw service in Nigeria. Trenchard learnt to fly in 1912. He was commander of the Royal Flying Corps on the Western Front from 1915 to 1917 and was briefly the RAF's first Chief of the Air Staff before commanding the Independent Air Force of bombers in France in 1918. Trenchard became Chief of the Air Staff again in 1919. He spent most of the 1920s establishing the RAF's status and future and was an advocate for the independent use of air power.

THE FIRST
TRANSATLANTIC FLIGHTS

In 1913, Lord Northcliffe, the owner of the *Daily Mail* offered a $10,000 prize for the first direct flight across the Atlantic. Glenn Curtiss built the flying boat *America* in order to make an attempt at the prize, but the outbreak of war put an end to preparations. During the war, the US Navy asked Curtiss to construct the NC flying boats, which in 1919 it decided to use to fly across the Atlantic in stages. Three flying boats set off on 8 May 1919 but only one, NC-4 under the command of Lieutenant Commander Albert C Read, completed the entire journey. Starting at Long Island and after stops at Chatham, Halifax (Novia Scotia), Tresspassy Bay (Newfoundland) and the Azores, the NC-4 landed at Lisbon in Portugal on 27 May after a 6,400-kilometre (4,000-mile) flight.

With Northcliffe's prize still unclaimed, five teams from British aircraft manufacturers set out to win it in 1919. A team from Shorts tried to fly east–west across the Atlantic but ditched into the sea on 18 April. The other teams from Martinsyde, Handley Page, Sopwiths and Vickers planned on starting from Newfoundland and flying west. The Sopwith Atlantic flown by Harry Hawker and Kenneth Mackenzie-Grieve took off on 18

May, but following engine problems, went down in the ocean well over half-way across. It was assumed the two men were dead, but miraculously the pair were picked up by a ship. The vessel did not have a radio so it was not until 25 May that the world heard Hawker and Mackenzie-Grieve had survived. They received a £5,000 cheque from Lord Northcliffe for their "magnificent failure". Two hours after Hawker and Mackenzie-Grieve departed, Freddie

LEFT British aviators Captain John Alcock (right) and Lieutenant Arthur Whitten-Brown at Clifden, Ireland after the first non-stop transatlantic flight by aeroplane in June 1919.

RIGHT US Navy Curtiss NC-4 which made the first crossing of the Atlantic in stages in May 1919. The NC-4's crew of six was commanded by Lieutenant Albert C Read.

Raynham and "Fax" Morgan's Martinsyde aircraft *Raymor* crashed on take-off, injuring Morgan and bringing their attempt at the prize to an end.

By 14 June, the Vickers team of pilot John Alcock and navigator Arthur Whitten Brown were ready to go in their modified Vickers Vimy. After a difficult take off in their over-loaded aircraft, they suffered a series of problems. The generator for the radio failed and their electrically heated suits did not work, making flying their open cockpit aircraft very difficult when they ran into bad

weather. Flying at night and disorientated by a storm, they nearly span into the sea when an engine stalled but Alcock managed to regain control. Flying on and into snow and hail, Brown had to climb out onto the wing to de-ice an engine. Frozen and exhausted, and

Harry Hawker
(1889–1921)

Australian Harry Hawker joined Tom Sopwith's fledgling aviation company at Brooklands in 1912 as a mechanic. Hawker quickly learnt to fly, set new records and worked on the Sopwith Tabloid. He continued with Sopwith as chief test pilot during the First World War and was involved in the design of many of the company's famous wartime aircraft including the Sopwith Pup and Camel. Sopwith Aviation went into liquidation in 1920. Hawker and Sopwith, with others, formed a new company which became known as Hawker Aircraft. Tragically, Hawker died in an air crash in 1921.

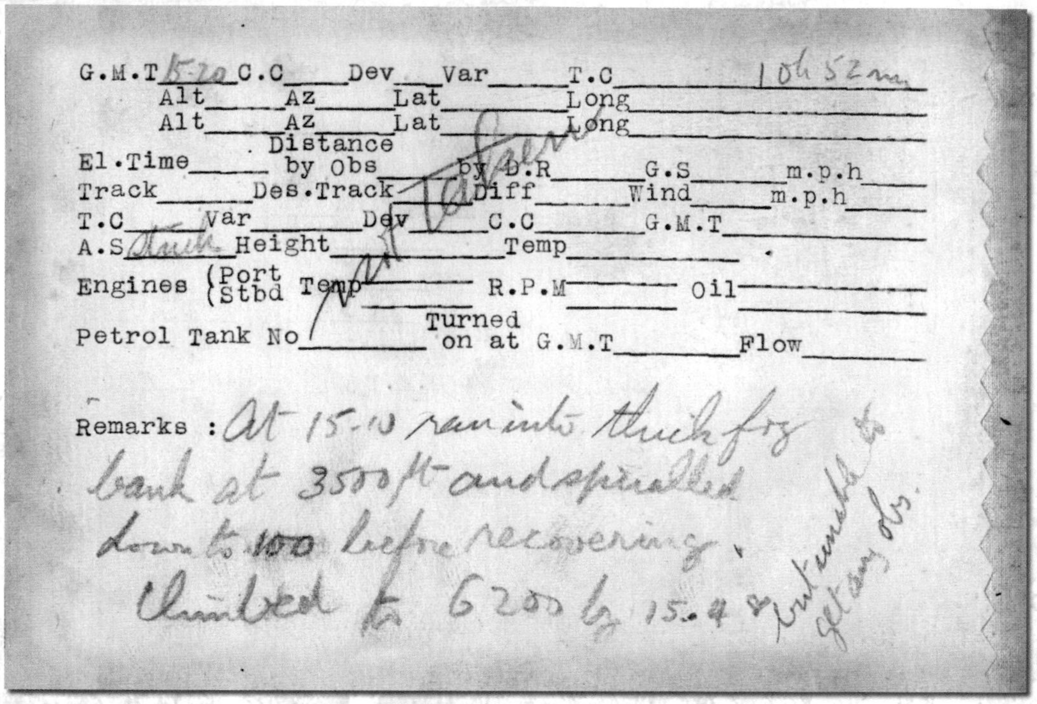

G.M.T 15-20 C.C ___ Dev ___ Var ___ T.C ___ 10h 52m
   Alt ___ Az ___ Lat ___ Long ___
   Alt ___ Az ___ Lat ___ Long ___
            Distance
El.Time ___ by Obs ___ by D.R ___ G.S ___ m.p.h
Track ___ Des.Track ___ Diff ___ Wind ___ m.p.h
T.C ___ Var ___ Dev ___ C.C ___ G.M.T ___
A.S ___ Height ___ Temp ___
Engines (Port Temp ___ R.P.M ___ Oil ___
        (Stbd
Petrol Tank No ___ Turned on at G.M.T ___ Flow ___

Remarks : At 15-10 ran into thick fog
bank at 3500 ft and spiralled
down to 100 before recovering.
Climbed to 6200 by 15.4 & not unable to
get any obs.

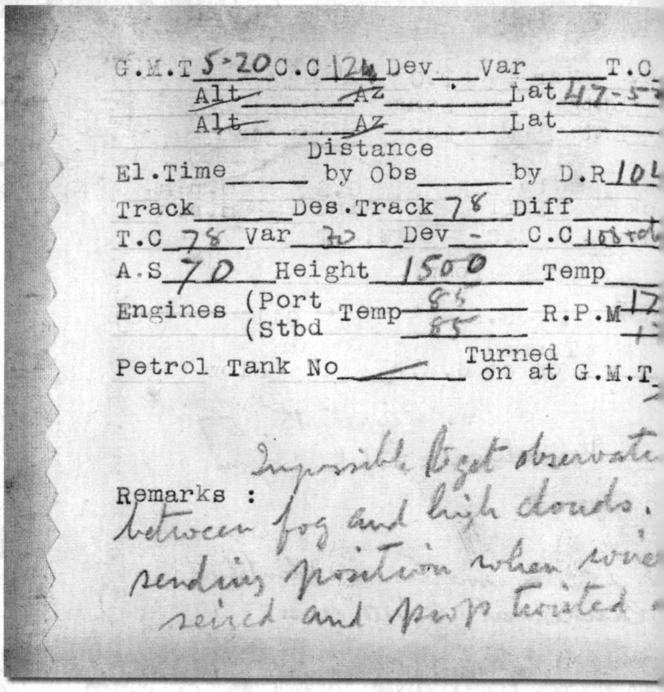

G.M.T 5-20 C.C 124 Dev ___ Var ___ T.C ___
   Alt ___ Az ___ Lat 47-5?
   Alt ___ Az ___ Lat ___
            Distance
El.Time ___ by Obs ___ by D.R 10?
Track ___ Des.Track 78 Diff ___
T.C 78 Var 30 Dev - C.C 10?
A.S 70 Height 1500 Temp ___
Engines (Port Temp 85 R.P.M 17
        (Stbd 85
Petrol Tank No ___ Turned on at G.M.T ___

Remarks : Impossible to get observation
between fog and high clouds.
sending position when wire?
seized and prop twisted

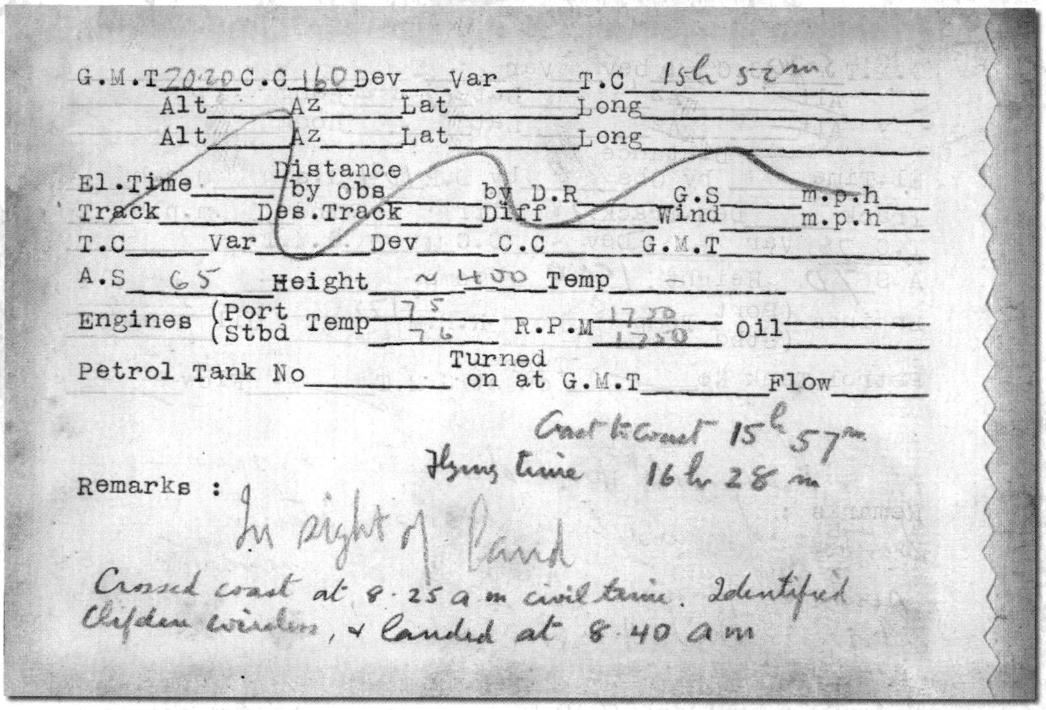

G.M.T 20-20 C.C 160 Dev ___ Var ___ T.C ___ 15h 52m
   Alt ___ Az ___ Lat ___ Long ___
   Alt ___ Az ___ Lat ___ Long ___
            Distance
El.Time ___ by Obs ___ by D.R ___ G.S ___ m.p.h
Track ___ Des.Track ___ Diff ___ Wind ___ m.p.h
T.C ___ Var ___ Dev ___ C.C ___ G.M.T ___
A.S 65 Height ~ 400 Temp - ___
Engines (Port Temp 75 R.P.M 1750 Oil ___
        (Stbd 76   1750
Petrol Tank No ___ Turned on at G.M.T ___ Flow ___

                    Coast to coast 15h 57m
                    Flying time 16h 28m
Remarks : In sight of land
Crossed coast at 8.25 a.m civil time. Identified
Clifden wireless, & landed at 8.40 a.m

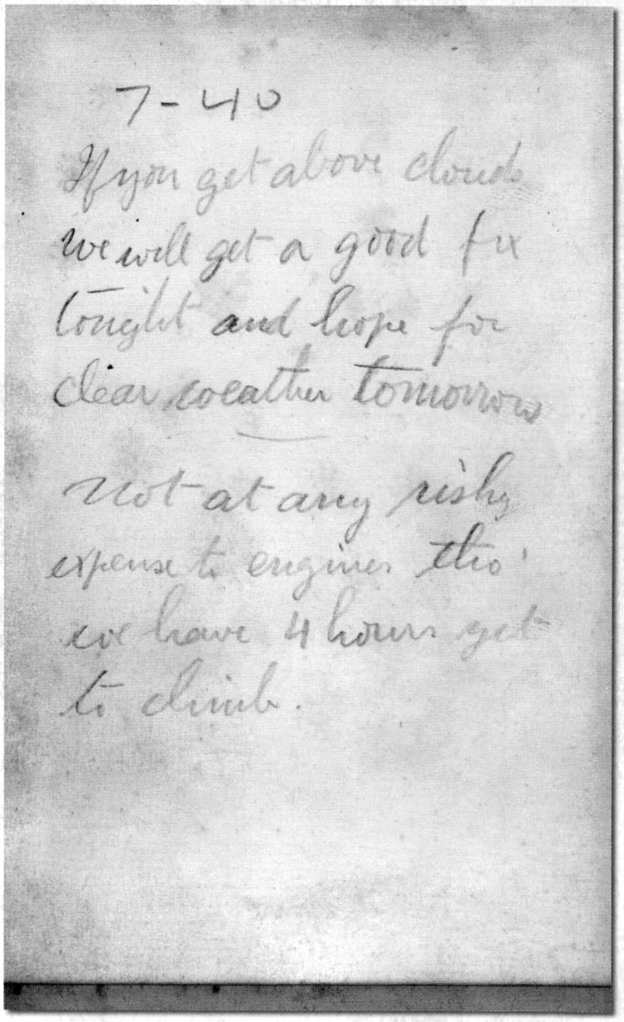

7-40

If you get above clouds
we will get a good fix
tonight and hope for
clear weather tomorrow

Not at any risky
expense to engines tho
we have 4 hours get
to climb.

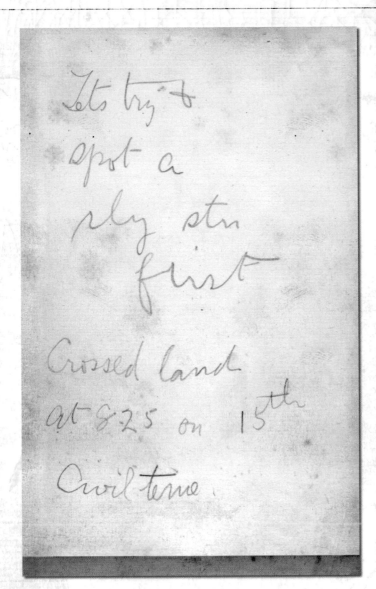

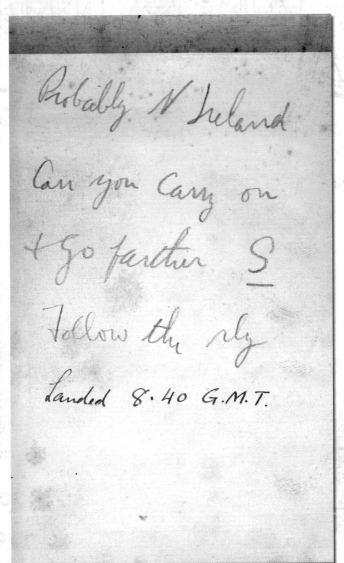

after more than 16 hours in the air, the two aviators were relieved to spot the coast of Ireland where they landed in marshy ground near Clifden. The Vimy tipped up on its nose at the end of its 3,115-kilometre- (1,936-mile-) flight, but both men emerged safely from the crash. Back in Newfoundland and with the Atlantic now conquered, the Handley Page team decided not to fly. Alcock and Brown received a hero's welcome in London as well as the prize for their flight which appeared to some to herald the imminent start of transatlantic air travel. However, it was to be 20 years before aircraft technology had moved on sufficiently for regular and reliable transatlantic passenger aeroplane flights to become established.

Zeppelins had already flown passenger flights in pre-war Germany, so airships seemed to offer the greatest potential for long-distance passenger travel by air. This was confirmed by the flight of British military airship R 34, which made the first double crossing of the Atlantic by air in July 1919. R 34 was virtually a copy of a captured Zeppelin which had been forced to land in Britain during the war. The airship, under the command of Major G H Scott and with a crew of 30, set off from East Fortune, Scotland on 2 July 1919. R 34 reached New York on 6 July having spent over 108 hours in the air and returned to Britain by 13 July after a total flight of 10,185 kilometres (6,330 miles). Passenger-carrying transatlantic Zeppelin flights commenced in 1928.

John Alcock and Arthur Whitten Brown

John Alcock (1892–1919) and Arthur Whitten Brown (1886–1948) both served in the Royal Flying Corps during the First World War. Coincidently both were shot down and spent time as prisoners of war but did not meet until Brown sought work at Vickers, where Alcock was a test pilot. They teamed up to make the first non-stop transatlantic aeroplane flight in 1919. Both were knighted in the same year and their Vickers Vimy was presented to the nation for display at the Science Museum in London on 15 December 1919. Alcock was killed three days later in a flying accident. Brown never flew again.

AVIATION
IN THE 1920S AND 1930S

In the years after the First World War, demand for aircraft was greatly reduced and, initially, manufacturers found continuing in business difficult. To survive, many were forced to produce alternative products, because air forces, struggling to find new roles in a more peaceful world, were severely cut back. Although engine power was steadily increased and more metal came to be used in aircraft construction, the machines that the military flew in the mid-1930s looked much the same as their First World War counterparts. Instead, it was to be civil aviation that saw the biggest developments. Initially, passenger aircraft were based on military designs; the first international daily scheduled passenger service in the world was established by Aircraft Transport and Travel in August 1919 with the flight by a de Havilland DH 16, a civilian version of the DH 9A bomber, between Hounslow, London and Le Bourget, Paris.

However, aircraft designed specifically for civil aviation soon replaced wartime types. These grew in numbers and sophistication and by the 1930s, large luxurious biplanes, sleek new monoplanes and colossal airships and flying boats were regularly criss-crossing the world along a network of air routes run by efficient airlines. Designers worked to build better performing aircraft which set new records for distance, speed and altitude. Air races attracted large crowds and record-breaking flights – and the pilots who made them – continued to capture the public's imagination. The Schneider Trophy race, a competition for seaplanes, was won by France in 1913 with an average speed of 74 kilometres per hour (46 miles per hour). A Supermarine S6B, designed by R J Mitchell, won the trophy for Britain in 1931 with a speed of 548.1 kilometres per hour (340.6 miles per hour), and went on to set a new world record of 655.8 kilometres per

LEFT An Aircraft Transport and Travel de Havilland DH 16 in 1919. Its four passengers each paid £21 for the flight from Hounslow, London to Le Bourget, Paris.

Alan Cobham
(1894–1973)

Alan Cobham learnt to fly in the RFC during the First World War. After a time with a company providing pleasure flights, he joined de Havilland Aeroplane Hire Service in 1921. His flights to Europe and North Africa in 1922, to Cape Town in 1924 and to Australia in 1926, helped to establish routes used by Imperial Airways. To encourage "air-mindedness" and aviation in the United Kingdom, in 1932 Cobham launched the National Aviation Day Campaign with a touring air display. A pioneer of in-flight refuelling, he set up Flight Refuelling Ltd in 1932.

LEFT Handing over a parcel to the US air mail service in 1925. Initially carrying mail was as commercially important to the airlines as transporting passengers.

BELOW The De Havilland DH 66 Hercules and the Armstrong Whitworth Argosy were Britain's Imperial Airways' main aircraft during the 1920s. Journeys along Imperial's empire routes could take several days and include overnight stops and various different modes of transport.

ABOVE Passengers waiting to board a Ford-Trimotor in the US. Made by Henry Ford from 1926, the Trimotor seated 13 passengers. Its three engines made it reliable but noisy and because of its all-metal body it became known as the "Tin Goose".

hour (407.5 miles per hour) showing how far aviation had progressed. Similarly, in 1924 two US Army Air Service Douglas World Cruisers were the first aircraft to travel completely round the world in an incredible 42,400-kilometre- (26,345-mile-) journey that took six months. Only seven years later in 1931, American Wiley Post and navigator Harold Gatty circled the globe in eight days and 16 hours in his Lockheed Vega *Winnie Mae*.

Other fliers such as Englishman Alan Cobham and Frenchman Jean Mermoz made their names by making route-proving flights for mail and passenger carrying services.

Trail-blazing flights could be very dangerous. In 1926, Cobham flew his DH 50 float plane to Australia and back but his mechanic Arthur Elliot was killed by a bullet fired from the ground whilst flying over Iraq. When Jean Mermoz went down in the desert in North Africa in 1926 he was held prisoner by tribesmen until a ransom was paid for his release. After many epic flights in South America in the late 1920s, Mermoz and the crew of his flying boat *La Croix du Sud* were lost over the South Atlantic in 1936.

For those who could afford them, passenger flights were not quite as hazardous, but in

ABOVE Passengers waiting to board a Ford-Trimotor in the US. Made by Henry Ford from 1926, the Trimotor seated 13 passengers. Its three engines made it reliable but noisy and because of its all-metal body it became known as the "Tin Goose".

Hélène Bouchier
(1908–1934)

French pilot Hélène Bouchier epitomized the true spirit of 1920s and '30s aviators. Bouchier learnt to fly in 1931 at the age of 23. In February 1933, she set out for to fly from Paris to Saigon but owing to mechanical problems her flight ended in Iraq. The outstanding aerobatic flying skills she demonstrated at the Villacoublay air show later that year brought Bouchier to the attention of the press and drew the admiration of aviation luminaries Jean Mermoz and Antoine de Saint-Exupéry. In August 1934, Bouchier set the woman's world speed record at 444 kilometres per hour (276 miles per hour) in a Caudron CL 450. She was killed during a training flight the following November.

BELOW Gladys Roy and Ivan Unger play tennis on the upper wings of a Curtiss JN-4 in October 1927. After the First World War, adventurous pilots bought up surplus military aircraft. Known as barnstormers, they travelled across the US thrilling audiences with dare-devil displays.

SEND YOUR GOODS OVERSEAS BY IMPERIAL AIRWAYS

Because

It will pay you to do so

It is the quickest method of transport

Simple packing is sufficient for even fragile goods

The freight rates are low, when the very rapid service is taken into consideration

Insurance rates for aerial travel are below those charged for surface transport

GOODS BY AIR TO ANYWHERE

You can send your goods to practically anywhere in Europe, Africa or India by Imperial Airways and they will arrive quicker than if sent by other means. Transport is not limited to places served directly by Imperial Airways. Goods are reforwarded from the nearest air port to their destination by the quickest means

1

SPEED

To Europe

Imperial Airways operates regular daily services to and from London, Paris, Brussels, Cologne and, in the summer, to and from Basle and Zürich. The air-liners fly at an average speed of 100 miles an hour and connect with other air services to the principal cities of Europe

To India and through Africa

Imperial Airways maintains weekly services to India and through Africa by means of which amazing savings in time can be effected. Indeed, to some destinations in Central Africa the time saved over other methods of transport amounts to as much as 40 days

SIMPLE PACKING— LESS HANDLING

Increasing quantities of merchandise are sent by Imperial Airways, not only for the sake of speed but also because the packing is much cheaper and simpler. Goods sent by air are most carefully handled, and there is no lifting by cranes or by dockhands and stevedores. Goods are placed in the holds of the aeroplanes by experts and travel smoothly to their destinations. Packing need not be elaborate or expensive. It need only be as strong as it should be for a short railway journey

2

DELICATE OBJECTS

This is why Imperial Airways has now become a large carrier of delicate objects : scientific instruments, wireless valves, watches, and so on. You can, however, send your heavy merchandise or your livestock equally easily by Imperial Airways and just as advantageously ; the Company has years of experience in the handling of goods

RATES

In addition to the advantages of speed and simple packing, Imperial Airways' freight rates are very reasonable. Particulars of tariffs for your class of goods will be given by Imperial Airways or by any shipping and forwarding agent. Examples of rates to different places overseas are given on page 8

LOW INSURANCE

The great freedom from damage or loss enjoyed by goods sent by Imperial Airways is reflected in the Insurance Rates. They are very much lower than those offered for any other form of transport—generally about *one-third* of the insurance premium levied on goods sent by surface transport

3

FACILITIES

A staff which is ... ling goods and ... as in the cleric... sent at every A... you much troub... are offered for ... drawbacks, clea... ment of Customs deposits, sh... bond and so on. Imperial Air... charges are based on the sam... adopted by shipping and for...

LONDON DELIV...

A well or... between Im... and its ... brings the ... London (Croydon) within ... delivery of the London area ... and deliver regularly through... calls are frequently made at ... terminal railway stations to c...

IMPERIAL AIRWAYS'

Imperial Airways publishes ... separately with each of its activ... full details and information ... here mentioned. These may ... request from Imperial Ai... Terminus, Victoria Station, ... phone Victoria 2211, from a... of Imperial Airways, or from a...

4

LIVESTOCK

By far the kindest and the best method of transporting livestock is by air. The speed of transit, the absence of transhipments, of long waits and of bumpings and joltings, lessens the distress from which animals suffer during surface travel. Our staff attends to their food and drink and to their general comfort throughout the journey and the animals or birds arrive in far better health and condition than when sent by any other method. This is of particular advantage in the case of animals intended for shows, where they are in competition with others still suffering from the effects of surface travel. Dogs, poultry, day-old chicks and even fish in tanks are carried by Imperial Airways on the European but not on the Empire routes. Very favourable insurance rates are quoted to give full cover on pets and other livestock

6

WHAT YOU CAN SEND BY AIR

Air travel is pre-eminently suitable for all kinds of goods that are required to arrive in first-class condition. The journeys occupy so little time that people are now sending even perishable goods to and from India and Africa. Eggs are sent by Imperial Airways in large quantities for hatching on farms abroad. Day-old chicks are carried in lots of one hundred each in cardboard boxes. Glassware, samples, fashion goods, scientific instruments, cinema films and equipment, motor cycles, spare parts and a hundred other kinds of goods are all frequently sent by air

WHY NOT SEND A TRIAL CONSIGNMENT?

Why not send a trial consignment of goods ? The great four-engined air-liners of Imperial Airways each have four freight compartments, each especially designed for a particular class of goods. Your first consignment will convince you of the advantages of sending freight by air

7

SAMPLES BY AIR ARRIVE FIRST

Business men gain a great deal by sending samples by air, especially along the Empire routes to India and through Africa. Transport by air will get samples and quotations into the hands of your customers days, and, in many instances, weeks, ahead of your competitors, and this gives you a great chance of securing the business

EXAMPLES OF TIMES AND RATES

Here are a few examples of Imperial Airways' freight rates and of the speed with which your packages travel. A consignment weighing 10 kilogrammes (22 lbs.) can be collected by Imperial Airways' van in London and delivered in the middle of Paris four hours later for 9s. 2d., or it can be delivered in Brussels in the same time and at about the same cost. The same consignment could be sent from London to Alexandria in 3½ days for £2, with 9d. extra for transport in London

8

IMPERIAL AI...

Airway Terminus: V... (opposite the Continental D... form), S.W.1

Telephone : Victoria 2211 (...
Telegrams : Impairlim Lon...

The Air Port of Londo...

Telephone : Croydon 2046 ...
Telegrams : Flying Croydo...

Paris: Airways House, 38, Ave ...

Telephone : Opéra 0916
Telegrams : Flying Paris

New York: The Plaza, F... 59th Street

Telephone : PL 3–0794 1740
Cables : Flying New York

Cairo: Heliopolis Aerodrome

Telephone : Zeitoun 1297-8
Telegrams : Airways Cairo

Karachi: Karachi Air Port

Telephone : Drigh Road 27
Telegrams : Airways Karachi

Cape Town: Wingfield Aero...

Telephone : Woodstock 993
Telegrams : Flying Cape Town

Printed by Henderson & Spalding, Ltd., Sylvan ... and published by Imperial Airways Limited, Air... S.W. 1, England.
IA/F/66. 20m. 3/33.

GOODS BY AIR AND RAIL

There is an arrangement with the British railway companies whereby merchandise may be carried at through rates from any railway station in Great Britain to places abroad served by Imperial Airways, and *vice versa*. Full particulars of this system are given in a leaflet *Rail and Air Transport*, which is obtainable from any main railway station in Great Britain or direct from Imperial Airways

BOOKINGS

As official agents we book for all Imperial Airways' services

5

SEND YOUR GOODS BY

IMPERIAL AIRWAYS

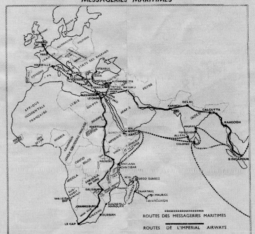

the 1920s with no heating, wicker seats, basic toilet facilities and travelling at heights that were badly affected by adverse weather conditions, flights were often cold and uncomfortable. With no insulation to deaden the sound of the engines, they were also extremely noisy. European airlines, developed with government subsidies and through mergers, began to grow into national airlines. Foremost amongst these was the German airline Lufthansa which in the 1930s was the world's largest, responsible for some 40 percent of global passenger air traffic. The French

ABOVE An Imperial Airways brochure promoting links between its African and Asian routes and those of the boat/train services of the French shipping line *Messageries Maritimes*.

OPPOSITE An 1930s Imperial Airways air freight brochure.

government subsidized a number of airlines which eventually became the state airline, Air France, in 1933. The British financed Imperial Airways became part of BOAC (British Overseas Airways Corporation) in 1939. With no state subsidies, airline development in America had to wait for the stimulus afforded by the privatization of the US Air Mail network in 1925.

NEW YORK TO PARIS
NON-STOP

Inspired by Alcock and Brown's transatlantic flight of 1919, French-born New York hotelier Raymond Orteig offered a $25,000 prize for the first flight from Paris to New York or New York to Paris, but it was not until the late 1920s that aircraft and aero engines capable of making the flight became available.

Charles Lindbergh was one of a number of entrants for the Orteig prize. He differed from the other competitors in that he opted to fly alone and in a single-engine aircraft called the *Spirit of St Louis* which was built to Lindbergh's specifications by the Ryan Aeronautical Company. It was powered by one of a new generation of very reliable engines; the radial Wright Whirlwind J-5C. Lindbergh took off from Roosevelt Field near New York at 7.52 a.m. on 20 May 1927. During his flight he encountered fog, storms, high-towering clouds and icy conditions. Fatigue was his biggest problem; he could not fall asleep for a moment as his aircraft was so unstable that it had to be controlled at all times, but he landed safely at Le Bourget, Paris, at 10.21 p.m. local time (5.21 p.m. New York time) on 21 May where he was greeted by some 100,000 people. He had flown more than 5,800 kilometres (3,600 miles) in 33-and-a-half hours. On 29 May he flew to Croydon, London and was met by a crowd of 150,000. Lindbergh's flight instantly shot him from obscurity to stardom; suddenly he was the most famous man in the world. On his return to the United States he was given a ticker-tape parade in front of three million New Yorkers and received a million telegrams, half a million letters and several thousand offers of marriage!

Other contenders for the Orteig Prize were not so fortunate. Flights prior to Lindbergh's took the lives of six aviators including the Frenchmen Charles Nungesser and François Colli. They took

LEFT Charles Lindbergh with his aircraft *Spirit of St Louis* before his flight from New York to Paris on 1 May 1927. Lindbergh's career prior to 1927, which included studying engineering at university, barnstorming, flying with the Army Air Service Reserve and serving as an airmail pilot, prepared him to meet the challenges of the flight.

OPPOSITE Lindbergh's *Spirit of St Louis* in flight. The aircraft was a specially commissioned modified Ryan NYP monoplane with an increased wingspan and the engine further forward than in the original design, so that a large fuel tank could be installed. Lindbergh was supported by a group of St Louis businessmen, to whom the aircraft owed its name.

Charles Lindbergh
(1902–1974)

Charles Lindbergh's 1927 first transatlantic solo flight made him internationally famous. The press named him "Lucky Lindy" and the "Lone Eagle". Showered with honours and idolised by millions, he was one of the twentieth century's first celebrities. In the late 1920s and 1930s he helped to promote the rapid development of US commercial aviation. He was opposed to US entry into the Second World War but after Pearl Harbor he worked and flew in combat as a civilian advisor. After the war he advised Pan Am on jet aircraft, including the Boeing 747. His book The *Spirit of St Louis* won a Pulitzer Prize in 1954.

off from Paris on 7 May 1927 but after crossing the French coast, were never seen again. However, a little more than a week after Lindbergh's flight, Clarence Chamberlain and Charles Levine successfully set a world distance record by flying between New York and Eisenben, Germany. On 1 July 1927, Richard Byrd and the crew of *America* flew as far as Paris but their attempts to land were frustrated by bad weather, leading them to ditch off the French coast after a flight of over 43 hours. Byrd and his crew survived but out of ten flyers involved in transatlantic attempts in the following two months, only two made it safely.

Flying across the Atlantic remained the great challenge for aviators during the 1930s. British pilot Jim Mollison made the first solo westward North Atlantic flight in 1932 in the de Havilland Puss Moth *Hearts Content* and made the first solo westward flight across the South Atlantic in the same aircraft in 1933. He flew the Atlantic again in that year together with his wife Amy Johnson, but the honour of being the first woman to fly across the Atlantic had already gone to Amelia Earhart in 1928 when she flew as a passenger with Wilmer Stultz and Lew

Gordon in the *Friendship*, a Fokker FVIIB-3m. Four years later she returned to the Atlantic and made the first solo flight by a woman in a Lockheed Vega Gull.

Lindbergh's flight and those of other the transatlantic pioneers were great personal triumphs but they also served to focus public attention on aviation and its great potential for personal transportation. Lindbergh's flight in particular, provoked huge interest in aviation in the United States and marked a revival in the fortunes of its struggling aircraft and air transport businesses.

LEFT The cramped cockpit of the *Spirit of St Louis*. With the fuel tank placed behind the engine, Lindbergh had no forward window so he either used a periscope or turned the aircraft in order to look out of the side windows.

OPPOSITE, ABOVE LEFT Amy Johnson kissing her husband Jim Mollison goodbye before his flight across the south Atlantic in 1933. The couple, together and singly, made many record-breaking flights in the 1930s. Amy Johnson died while flying with the British Air Transport Auxiliary in 1941.

OPPOSITE, RIGHT ABOVE AND BELOW Congratulatory message from Louis Blériot, and from Charles and Anne Lindbergh to Amy Johnson after she became the first woman to fly solo from Britain to Australia in May 1930.

OPPOSITE, BELOW LEFT Amelia Earhart; the first woman to cross the Atlantic by aeroplane in June 1928. Earhart and her navigator Fred Noonan disappeared over the Pacific during a round-the-world flight in 1937.

James Mollison
(1905–1959)

Scotsman "Jim" Mollison set many aviation records in the 1930s. He learnt to fly at RAF Duxford and when he obtained his commission in the RAF at the age of 18 he was the youngest officer in the service. On leaving the RAF he set out to make his name in civil aviation. Long distance flying was a way of doing this and in 1931 and 1932 he set record times for flights to Australia and South Africa. He met and married the famous aviator Amy Johnson, in 1932. Mollison made the first west to east transatlantic flights against the much more challenging prevailing winds in 1932 and 1933.

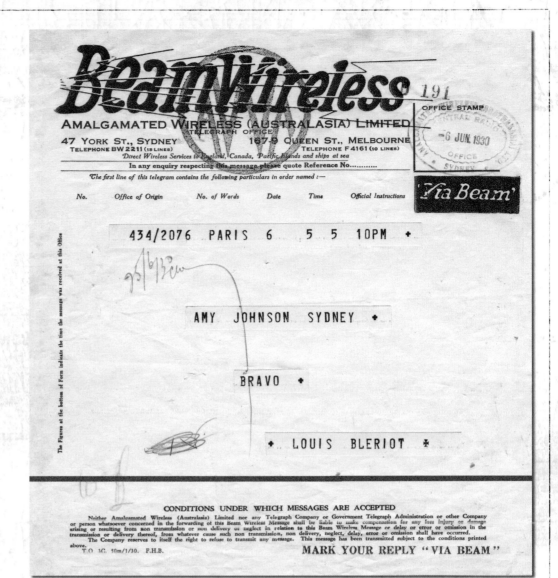

Beam Wireless

AMALGAMATED WIRELESS (AUSTRALASIA) LIMITED
TELEGRAPH OFFICE.
47 YORK ST., SYDNEY   167-9 QUEEN ST., MELBOURNE
TELEPHONE BW 2211 (15 LINES)   TELEPHONE F 4161 (10 LINES)
Direct Wireless Services to England, Canada, Pacific Islands and ships at sea

In any enquiry respecting this message please quote Reference No............

The first line of this telegram contains the following particulars in order named :—

No.	Office of Origin	No. of Words	Date	Time	Official Instructions

'Via Beam'

434/2076 PARIS 6 5 5 10PM +

AMY JOHNSON SYDNEY +

BRAVO +

+ LOUIS BLERIOT +

CONDITIONS UNDER WHICH MESSAGES ARE ACCEPTED

Neither Amalgamated Wireless (Australasia) Limited nor any Telegraph Company or Government Telegraph Administration or other Company or person whatsoever concerned in the forwarding of this Beam Wireless Message shall be liable to make compensation for any loss injury or damage arising or resulting from non transmission or non delivery or neglect in relation to this Beam Wireless Message or delay or error or omission in the transmission or delivery thereof, from whatever cause such non transmission, non delivery, neglect, delay, error or omission shall have occurred. The Company reserves to itself the right to refuse to transmit any message. This message has been transmitted subject to the conditions printed above.
T.O 3C. 50m/1/30. F.H.B.

MARK YOUR REPLY "VIA BEAM"

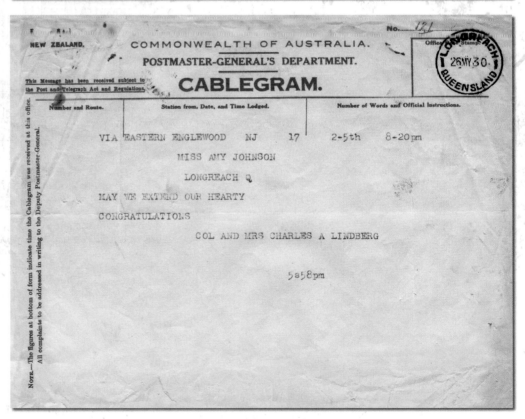

No. 121

NEW ZEALAND.   COMMONWEALTH OF AUSTRALIA.
POSTMASTER-GENERAL'S DEPARTMENT.

This Message has been received subject to the Post and Telegraph Act and Regulations.

CABLEGRAM.

Number and Route.	Station from, Date, and Time Lodged.		Number of Words and Official Instructions.

VIA EASTERN ENGLEWOOD NJ 17 | 2-5th 8-20pm

MISS AMY JOHNSON

LONGREACH Q

MAY WE EXTEND OUR HEARTY

CONGRATULATIONS

COL AND MRS CHARLES A LINDBERG

5 as 58pm

AÉRO-CLUB DE FRANCE

COMMISSION D'AVIATION — 35, Rue François-1er, 35 — PARIS

PROCÈS-VERBAL (1)

New York - Paris.   Record de distance en ligne droite
Prix Raymond Orteig

RENSEIGNEMENTS DIVERS

Nom du Commissaire agréé responsable.

Ingénieur en Chef Hirschauer —
Secrétaire de la Commission sportive de
l'Aéro-Club de France

Noms des autres Commissaires agréés.

Noms des Commissaires-Adjoints.

Membre de (2)

Nom du (des) chronométreur.

Description du terrain de l'épreuve (3).

Port Aérien du Bourget — Paris.

---

(1). — Indiquer la nature de la manifestation sportive ou du record.

Le procès-verbal doit être adressé dans les 24 heures de la fin de l'épreuve à « l'Aéro-Club de France ».

(2). — Indiquer de quelle Société font partie les Commissaires. Indiquer si le contrôle est assuré par « l'Aéro-Club de France » ou par une Société déléguée à cet effet.

(3). — Donner la description sommaire de la piste ; y joindre un croquis schématique côté, qui pourra être utilement établi à la page 4 de ce procès-verbal, indiquant les principales dimensions, l'emplacement des poteaux, leurs distances respectives, etc.

Indiquer le sens de la marche (main à laquelle marchent les concurrents).

Indiquer avec PRÉCISION comment le Commissaire a effectué la mesure de la piste.

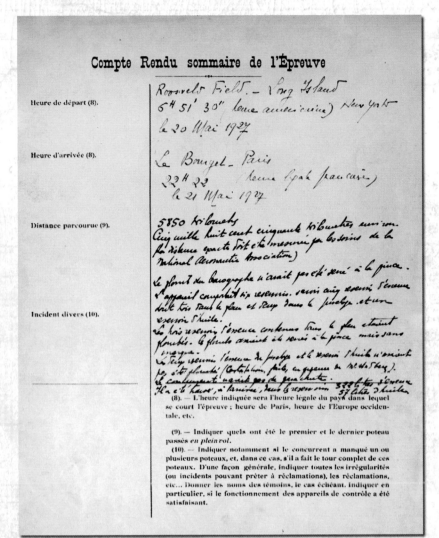

Compte Rendu sommaire de l'Épreuve

Heure de départ (8).

Heure d'arrivée (8).

Distance parcourue (9).

Incident divers (10).

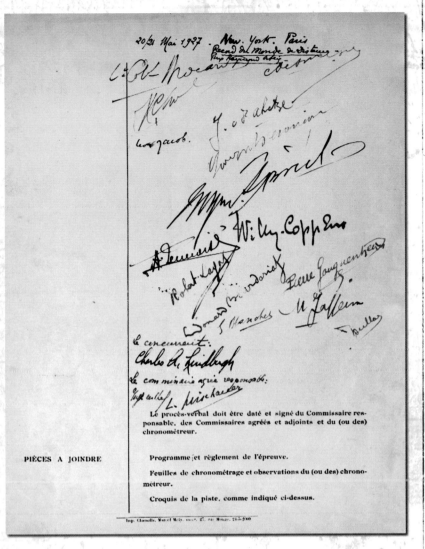

PIÈCES A JOINDRE

Le procès-verbal doit être daté et signé du Commissaire responsable, des Commissaires agréés et adjoints et du (ou des) chronométreur.

Programme et règlement de l'épreuve.

Feuilles de chronométrage et observations du (ou des) chronométreur.

Croquis de la piste, comme indiqué ci-dessus.

OPPOSITE AND ABOVE The official report issued by the *Aéro-Club de France* recording Charles Lindbergh's record-breaking transatlantic flight from New York to Paris in 1927.

RIGHT The $25,000 Raymond Orteig prize won by Charles Lindbergh for the first non-stop flight from Paris to New York in 1927.

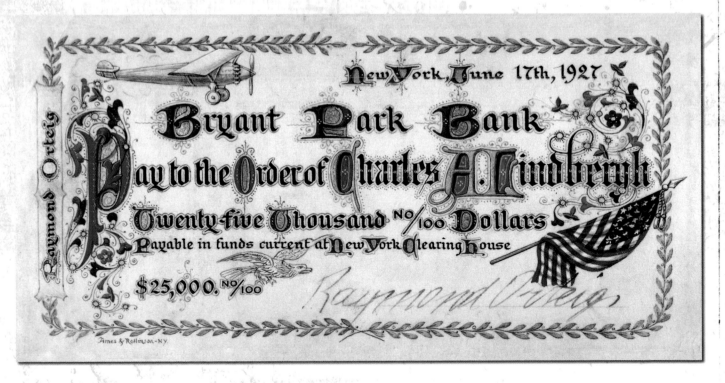

AIRSHIPS
AND FLYING BOATS

After the R 34's transatlantic flights in 1919, many people believed that airships offered the best option for long-distance passenger flights. Although the German Zeppelin company had considerable experience in building and operating airships, restrictions set in place by the post-First World War treaties made it difficult for the company to operate until, under the inspired leadership of Hugo Eckener, it succeeded in winning a contract in 1922 to build the USS *Los Angeles* for the US Navy. Zeppelin formed an alliance with the American company Goodyear, producing two further airships for the US Navy, both of which were later lost over the sea.

In the late 1920s, Britain created two large airships, the R 100 and the R 101 for use on routes to Canada, India and Australia. The R 100, designed by Barnes Wallis and built by Vickers, made a successful inaugural flight to Canada in 1930 but after the loss of the R 101, which crashed in France on a flight headed for India in October 1930, R 100 was scrapped and Britain abandoned the concept for good. With both French and Italian craft suffering similar fates, only the Germans retained their faith in airships.

Their confidence appeared to be vindicated by the launch of the *Graf Zeppelin* in September 1928. Her flight from Germany to New York the next month saw the beginning of a successful ten-year career. Her trips across the Atlantic, to South America in particular, constituted the only long-range passenger air service at that time. *Graf Zeppelin*'s successor, the *Hindenburg* was designed to carry 50 passengers in luxury across the North Atlantic. At 245 metres (803 feet) long and with a maximum diameter of 41 metres (135 feet), the *Hindenburg* was the biggest aircraft ever to fly. She made ten successful round trans-Atlantic trips to the United States in 1936, but burst into flames as she came in to land at Lakehurst, New Jersey at the end of her first flight of 1937 to the US. Miraculously, 62 of the 97 people on

Hugo Eckener
(1868–1954)

Hugo Eckener joined Zeppelin in 1906 as a publicist, but due to his natural aptitude for flying, he soon became an airship captain and during the First World War trained many Zeppelin pilots. After the war, as the head of Luftschiffbau Zeppelin, Eckener was instrumental in raising public support for airships and personally commanded the *Graf Zeppelin* on most of its record-setting journeys, including the first round-the-world passenger-carrying flight in the summer of 1929. Eckener always made safety his top priority and under him Zeppelin enjoyed a perfect operational record. This ended with the *Hindenburg* disaster of 1937 but by then Eckener, an ardent anti-Nazi, had been sidelined by Hitler's regime.

ABOVE LZ 129 *Hindenburg* engulfed in flames on its arrival at Lakenhurst, New Jersey on 6 May 1937. The exact cause of the tragedy has never been fully established.

LEFT Zeppelin LZ 127 *Graf Zeppelin* over New York in August 1934. The Zeppelins could cross the Atlantic in approximately two days. Their passengers travelled in very comfortable accommodation including private cabins, lounges, dining rooms and observation decks.

board survived the inferno but the disaster spelt the end of international airship travel.

As a result, flying boats remained the only aircraft suitable for long-range passenger transport over the world's oceans. As they could take off from and land on water, there was no need for long runways or complex airfields, both of which were difficult and expensive to construct, particularly in remote locations.

In the 1930s, Pan American or "Pan Am" became the preferred overseas airline of the US government. Under the dynamic direction of Juan Trippe, Pan Am set up routes in the early 1930s from the USA to the Caribbean and South America. Trippe then turned his attention to establishing routes across the Pacific. In October 1936, Pan Am's Martin 130 Philippine Clipper set off from California for the first scheduled trans-Pacific passenger flight. With scheduled stops on the way, the flying boat arrived in Hong Kong three days later.

In Europe, the French Latécoère operated flying boats over the Mediterranean and on South Atlantic mail flights. Lufthansa also introduced a Europe to South America mail service in 1934 using Dornier Wals, which stopped at a ship stationed in mid-ocean to

Boeing 314 Clipper

With a 5,600-kilometres (3,500-mile) range, the Boeing 314 made its first transatlantic scheduled passenger flight in June 1939. The 314 was probably the most luxurious airliner ever built and for over 30 years, the largest commercial aircraft. It was capable of carrying 74 passengers seated or 40 in sleeping berths. Accommodation included a dining saloon that could be transformed into a lounge, plus a deluxe compartment that was offered as a bridal suite. Twelve of these wonderful aircraft were built between 1938 and 1941. They were drafted into wartime use and among the VIPs they carried were US President Franklin D Roosevelt and British Prime Minister Winston Churchill.

re-fuel. Britain had used a mixture of flying boats, land-planes and trains on its routes to South Africa and Australia for a number of years but in 1937, Imperial Airways introduced the Short S-23 C-Class or Empire flying boats which flew in stages from Southampton to Cape Town and Sydney.

Pan Am's Clippers and Imperial's Empire flying boats were noted both for their high standards of passenger service and for their well-appointed accommodation. In May 1939, Juan Trippe introduced the most luxurious of all the flying boats, the Boeing 314, on to northern transatlantic routes, but the outbreak of the

Second World War in Europe put an end to Pan Am's fledgling service. Although they continued to be used during the war, the construction of numerous airfields throughout the world, together with the development of land-planes with far longer flying ranges, effectively brought the flying boat era to an end.

LEFT Passengers boarding a Pan Am Boeing Clipper flying boat.

BELOW An Imperial Airways poster featuring an "Empire" or Short S-23 C-class flying boat. *Canopus*, the first C-Class, made its initial flights in 1936.

THE FIRST
MODERN AIRLINERS

In 1918, the US Army Air Service initiated the world's first regular airmail service between Washington and New York. During the following year, the US Post Office took over and built a transcontinental service using its own pilots and aircraft and by 1924, had a continent-wide system of lights to guide aircraft at night. As a result, the mail could be flown across the US in 30 hours, compared to the three days it took by train.

This network was subsequently handed over to commercial operators and many small companies, such as the Robertson Aircraft Corporation, for whom Charles Lindbergh flew, started to carry mail. Lindbergh rose to fame in 1927 when he made the first solo flight across the Atlantic, an achievement that gave a tremendous boost to aviation in the US. New airlines rapidly developed. Soon carrying passengers as well as mail was a commonplace thing. By 1930, the "Big Four" – American Airlines, United Air Lines, Eastern Airlines and Transcontinental and Western Air, dominated US domestic routes.

At the heart of this change were a number of new aircraft; the tough Ford, Fokker and Boeing trimotors with their three engines, one on each wing and another on the nose. These aircraft may have been fast, but they were also uncomfortable. But an even greater revolution was on the horizon with the advent of a new generation of sleek, aerodynamic all-metal monoplane airliners powered by increasingly efficient air-cooled radial engines. United Airlines led the way in 1933 with the introduction of the 250-kilometre-per-hour (155-mile-per-hour) Boeing 247 which could carry ten passengers in reasonable comfort in its soundproofed cabin. The 247 was so advanced that United's rivals were forced to replace their existing fleets and they turned to the Douglas Aircraft Company, who devised the DC series of aircraft. The DC-1 of 1933 was quickly followed by the DC-2. Superior to the 247, this was superseded in turn by the 290-kilometre-per-hour (180-mile-per-hour), 21-seat DC-3 in 1936. With the introduction of the DC-3 and improvements in radio, radio-based navigation and flying with instruments in poor visibility, US airlines were finally able offer a reliable service that could make money just from transporting passengers. Reduced fares encouraged more people to fly and by the late 1930s the DC-3 was carrying over 90 per cent of the three million or so American passengers travelling by air each year.

BELOW LEFT TWA was one of the first US airlines to purchase the Douglas DC-3. TWA passengers travelled both on business and to vacation destinations.

Howard Hughes
(1905–1976)

A wealthy industrialist, aviator, film director, producer and philanthropist, Howard Hughes learnt to fly in 1927 and founded the Hughes Aircraft Company in 1934 to make the H-1 racer in which he set a world land-plane speed record of 566.9 kilometres per hour (352.32 miles per hour) in 1935. In 1938 he set another record by flying around the world in a Lockheed 14 Super Electra in just over 91 hours, and in 1941 took control of Transcontinental and Western Air, later known as Trans World Airlines (TWA). 1947 saw the one and only flight of his famous wartime H-4 Hercules transport aircraft Spruce Goose. Suffering from worsening obsessive-compulsive disorder and increasingly surrounded by controversy, Hughes died an eccentric recluse in 1976.

ABOVE An Imperial Airways Handley Page HP42. These large biplanes carried 24 passengers on Empire and European routes from 1930 until almost the end of the decade. Travelling at a steady 161 kilometres per hour (100 miles per hour) they gained a reputation for both safety and reliability.

RIGHT Passengers leave an Imperial Airways Armstrong Whitworth AW Ensign. Although modern in appearance and equipped with a spacious cabin, the Ensign did not compare with contemporary American designs.

In contrast to the DC-3, European designs lagged far behind. The Handley Page HP42 introduced by Imperial Airways in 1930 was a giant biplane which carried 24 passengers at a stately 161 kilometres per hour (100 miles per hour) on the airline's Empire and European routes. Newer designs followed, such as the all-metal stressed skin Armstrong Whitworth AW27 Ensign and de Havilland's beautiful DH 91 Albatross, which entered service just before the outbreak of the Second World War.

LEFT An American Airlines Douglas DC-3 in flight.

By the late 1930s, US air passengers could travel in properly heated, soundproofed comfort, attended by stewardesses or stewards, serving in-flight drinks and meals, with beds even being provided on the more lavish services. However, the problem of turbulence created by adverse weather conditions remained. The solution was to fly higher into the realms of the weather-free stratosphere. Boeing's B-307 Stratoliner of 1938 was the first airliner capable of doing this. With its pressurized cabin and turbo supercharged engines which could work efficiently at such increased heights, it indicated the direction that commercial aviation was to take.

Douglas DC-3

The Douglas DC-3 was the most successful aircraft of its day and indeed, many would argue that it is the greatest of all time. Design work on the DC-3 began in 1934 at the request of American Airlines who wanted a longer DC-2 to carry more passengers, plus another version with sleeping berths. The 14-berth Douglas Skysleeper was soon eclipsed by the standard 21-seat DC-3 which was both comfortable and very reliable. It could operate from concrete, grass and even dirt surfaces and its crews considered it to be virtually indestructible. In addition to the 455 DC-3s made, 10,174 of the C-47 military version were also produced, some of which are still flying today.

ABOVE An American Airlines DC-3 parked on the tarmac at La Guardia airport, New York City in the 1940s.

LEFT Passengers boarding a Boeing 247 at Boeing Field in Seattle. With its streamlined all-metal, cantilevered wing design and retractable undercarriage, the Boeing 247 was the first true modern airliner, but it was soon to be upstaged by Douglas's DC-2 and DC-3.

THE APPROACH AND
OUTBREAK OF THE SECOND WORLD WAR

Whilst the development of passenger flight continued, the military value of aircraft had not been forgotten, but there was by no means consensus on how best they should be employed. In Britain, a role was found for the RAF in "policing the Empire" (keeping the peace in the colonies). In France, the perennial fear of German militarism provided justification for maintaining an air force, and in Italy the rise of Mussolini prompted the expansion of that country's air arm to support its own imperial plans. In the United States, the focus was on defence, while Japan began to build a carrier fleet. But it was to be Germany whose air force (the Luftwaffe) would shape the development of air power in the 1930s, leading other nations to re-arm as Hitler's territorial ambitions became increasingly apparent.

Germany was forbidden by the terms of the Treaty of Versailles from having an air force. However, in the 1920s, an agreement with the Soviet Union meant that it secretly continued to train military pilots there. Aircraft development continued too, often under the guise of building for commercial aviation. In 1933, when Hitler and the Nazis took power, Germany began to re-arm more swiftly, soon unveiling its air force, the Luftwaffe, to the world. More pilots commenced training and the German aircraft industry began to produce new combat aircraft which were at the cutting edge of modern design. By the mid-1930s, biplane aircraft were being replaced by monoplanes such as the Messerschmitt Bf 109 fighter.

The Luftwaffe proved the effectiveness of its aircraft, tactics and personnel during the Spanish Civil War (1936–1939), when the Condor Legion was despatched to Spain to fight on the Nationalist (Fascist) side. The Bf 109 outfought the Republican Soviet-designed fighters, and the Legion began to carry out close air-support operations, working with the army on the ground to destroy enemy troop concentrations and communications. A valuable lesson was learned in the use of aircraft as "aerial artillery", although it was the attack by German aircraft on Guernica in April 1937 that came to symbolize the German involvement in the war, and seemed to prove the awesome destructive power of the bomber against civilian targets.

Erhard Milch
1892–1972

Milch did more than any other individual to shape the development of the Luftwaffe. He was born in Wilhelmshaven, served as a fighter pilot in the First World War and joined the German national airline, Lufthansa, in 1926. An early supporter of the Nazi party, Milch was Hermann Göring's deputy at the air ministry and he organized the construction of the Luftwaffe at a time when Germany was forbidden to have an air force. He commanded forces during the invasion of Norway in 1940, and was instrumental in increasing aircraft production from late 1941 onwards. He was sentenced to life imprisonment at the Nuremberg Trials in 1947, but this was later commuted to 15 years.

ABOVE Guernica, Spain, after it had been attacked by the Luftwaffe in 1937. Guernica came to symbolize the horror of aerial attack on civilians and inspired one of the most powerful works of art to emerge from war – Pablo Picasso's painting of the same name.

BELOW Adolf Hitler and his senior commanders watch a flypast of German aircraft in 1935. The Luftwaffe was a vital part of German battle strategy.

When Germany invaded and conquered Poland in September 1939, it heralded to the world that a new form of warfare had arrived. Blitzkrieg, or "Lightning War", involved tanks and mechanized infantry advancing at breathtaking speed through enemy defences that had been smashed by the aerial artillery – specifically Ju 87 Stuka dive bombers. This type of combat did not rely on huge numbers of aircraft or highly advanced technology. Concentration of force and speed of action were key, as was achieving air superiority over the battlefield.

When the Germans invaded France, the British and French commanders also found themselves outmanoeuvred, just like the Polish military. Firstly airfields were attacked, crippling the Allies' ability to maintain air superiority. Although fighters such as the Hawker Hurricane were able to match the German aircraft in terms of performance, others such as the Morane-Saulnier MS 406 were not up to the job. As the German army advanced westwards, with the Luftwaffe spearheading the attack, allied squadrons were forced to retreat. The aircraft with which the RAF counter-attacked, such as the Bristol Blenheim and Fairey Battle light bomber, achieved little. Many were destroyed, and pre-war trained airmen lost.

By the summer of 1940, Germany was in control of continental Europe from Poland through to the English Channel, partly because of the innovative use of air power. Only the miraculous evacuation of the British Expeditionary Force and remnants of the French army at Dunkirk prevented the German victory from being overwhelming and absolute.

Junkers Ju 87 Stuka

No aircraft is more associated with Blitzkrieg than the Ju 87 Stuka. The "lightning war" strategy centred on tanks and mechanized infantry receiving close support by "aerial artillery"– in particular, the Ju 87. The Stuka (the name was derived from *Sturzkampfflugzeug*, meaning dive-bomber) entered service in 1937. A notable modification to the aircraft was the addition of sirens to the landing gears, which caused the Stuka to emit a distinctive wail as it dived. Despite its devastating early performance, its slow speed made it vulnerable to fighter attack. After the Battle of Britain in 1940, when large numbers of Ju 87s were shot down, their effectiveness markedly decreased, and although they continued in service, they never again enjoyed the same level of success.

OPPOSITE, ABOVE The German invasion of Poland, September 1, 1939. A key component of Blitzkrieg was the aerial artillery provided by the Luftwaffe. 890 bombers were deployed by the German air force in the campaign and Poland was overwhelmed within a month by rapidly moving ground forces supported by aircraft.

OPPOSITE, BELOW Shanghai being bombed by Japanese aircraft. In the 1930s Japan used its aircraft as a way to attack the morale of Chinese civilians. The bombing of Shanghai in 1932 was one of the first uses of carrier-based bombers in the Pacific.

STURZKAMPF FLUGZEUG
JUNKERS-
JU 87

MIT JUNKERS-HOCHLEISTUNGS-
FLUGMOTOR

THE BATTLE OF BRITAIN
AND THE BLITZ

"What General Weygand called the Battle of France is over. I expect that the Battle of Britain is about to begin." With those words, British Prime Minister Winston Churchill announced that the United Kingdom could expect the full force of the Nazi war machine, which had swept largely unchecked across Europe, to be directed across the English Channel. Hitler ordered his air force to achieve air superiority over the United Kingdom as a necessary prelude to invasion.

Defending the British Isles from the threat of the bomber became a high priority for military planners. An intricate early-warning system was in place, based on the principles of defence established during the First World War. Well organized command and control was augmented by the latest scientific miracle – radar – assisted by the more traditional teams of observers on the ground ready to report incoming aircraft. The RAF did not have as many aircraft or pilots as the Luftwaffe but it had a simple task: to remain in being. Unless the Germans could destroy the United Kingdom's ability to defend itself from the air, the invasion could not take place.

The battle for aerial supremacy, which became known as the Battle of Britain, began in June 1940 with sporadic attacks by the Luftwaffe over the Channel. These intensified in July. Then, on 13 August, massive fleets of German bombers and their escorting fighters attacked the bases, radar installations and centres of aircraft production that were vital to the defences. The pilots of the RAF came from the UK, the Commonwealth, occupied Europe and the United States, and they fought doggedly and determinedly to stem the tide. Luftwaffe attacks increasingly began to focus on the airfields, in an attempt to destroy the Allies' Spitfires and Hurricanes on the ground and deprive them of the bases from which the defence was maintained.

These attacks proved effective for the Luftwaffe but although the RAF was hard-pressed, it was able to hang on. Then in September, the Luftwaffe turned its attention to London. This provided respite for the RAF. By October, it was clear that the Luftwaffe would not achieve air superiority over Britain. It would

ABOVE Pilots of No. 610 Squadron Royal Air Force between sorties at RAF Hawkinge, Kent, 1940. Squadrons were held at different states of readiness, ranging from "available" (ready to take off in 20 minutes) to "stand-by" (two minutes). Once the call to "scramble" was given, the pilots would run to their aircraft, knowing that every second gained could give them more time to climb to a good altitude for attack. During the heaviest days of fighting, squadrons could be called into action several times, pausing only to re-arm and refuel.

RIGHT The Messerschmitt Bf 109. Designed by engineer Willy Messerschmitt, over 30,000 109s of various different marks were built. The 109, one of the first all-metal monoplanes to enter service, was small, light, fast and manoeuvrable. The small cockpit did not give the pilot a good view, and it was difficult to handle at low speeds, but it proved to be a very capable fighter.

RIGHT Hawker Hurricanes of No. 501 Squadron, Gravesend, 14 September 1940. Designed by Sydney Camm, the Hurricane was part of the first generation of monoplane fighters, and it entered service in 1937. Like the Spitfire, the Hurricane was fitted with the Rolls-Royce Merlin engine.

BELOW Supermarine Spitfire Mk IAs of No. 610 Squadron. This variant of Spitfire was armed with eight Browning .303 inch machine guns. Later marks were fitted with cannons (firing explosive shells, rather than small rifle bullets) which after some early problems, proved much more effective. Key to the Spitfire's success was its innovative design and powerful, reliable Rolls-Royce Merlin engine.

OVERLEAF St Paul's Cathedral stands above the surrounding burning buildings during the Blitz. Winston Churchill was aware of the powerful national symbolism provided by the survival of the iconic building, stating during the Blitz that "At all costs, St Paul's must be saved".

instead concentrate on bombing British cities by night, in what became known as the "Blitz". The RAF had effectively ended the threat of invasion. It was, as Churchill had predicted, "their finest hour".

But the cities continued to suffer. The German attacks were the first real sustained attempt to test British Prime Minister Stanley's Baldwin's theory that "the bomber will always get through", and see whether civilian morale would crack under the pressure of aerial bombardment. Until May 1941, bombers such as the Heinkel He 111 and Junkers Ju 88 attempted to batter London into submission. They were guided by very sophisticated navigation systems, and had considerable success avoiding British anti-aircraft defences. 10 May saw the largest number of casualties, when over 1,400 civilians were killed. The Blitz meant that thousands of ordinary men and women had a role to play in defending the nation, in both military and civilian capacities. They worked as first aiders, air raid wardens and firefighters and manned anti-aircraft batteries and barrage balloon defences.

German attacks lessened as Hitler turned his attention to the Russian front, but raids on

Sir Hugh Dowding
(1882–1970)

Dowding was made Commander-in-Chief of RAF Fighter Command in 1936. Until the outbreak of war, he worked tirelessly to prepare Britain's air defences against the attack that many felt was inevitable. These included the development of the "Chain Home" radar network, and the perfecting of the command and control systems that would prove so valuable during the Battle of Britain. Dowding refused to allow the dispersal of his Spitfire squadrons during the ill-fated Norwegian campaign and the Battle of France in 1940 and successfully managed the resources at his disposal during the Battle of Britain itself. To him must go a great deal of the credit for victory.

Britain continued sporadically. Then in 1944, a new weapon was introduced – the pilotless V1 flying bomb. In the summer of that year, around 100 V1s were sent across the Channel every day, proving difficult to intercept thanks to their size and speed. V1s were followed by the even more deadly V2 ballistic missiles, which were impossible to intercept. The RAF made enormous efforts to destroy these

weapons at source, by bombing their launch sites and production centres.

The Blitz on London and other British cities was a horrendous demonstration of the power of the bomber. But at no point did it seriously threaten to destroy British morale. And the scale of the German effort would be dwarfed by what was to follow: the enormous Allied strategic bombing campaign.

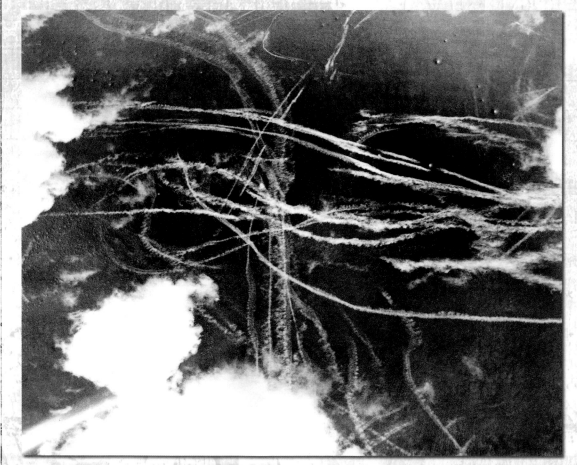

OPPOSITE An extract from Pilot Officer Michael Christopher Bindloss Boddington's logbook, covering the period 2 August–11 September 1940. Boddington, from Hawkshead, Lancashire, flew with No. 234 Squadron during the Battle of Britain. He joined the Royal Air Force Volunteer Reserve (RAFVR) in 1936 and after the Battle went on to command squadrons in North Africa, Malta and Sicily.

LEFT The pattern of condensation trails left by British and German aircraft after a dog fight. Before the war the RAF's tactics were based on the idea that unescorted bombers would be the target for the defending fighters. Formations were rigidly organized, and it was thought unlikely that there would be much fighter-against-fighter combat. However, the pilots' experiences in the Battle of France and the early stages of the Battle of Britain forced tactics to change, leading to intense dogfighting as fighters manoeuvred desperately to bring their guns to bear.

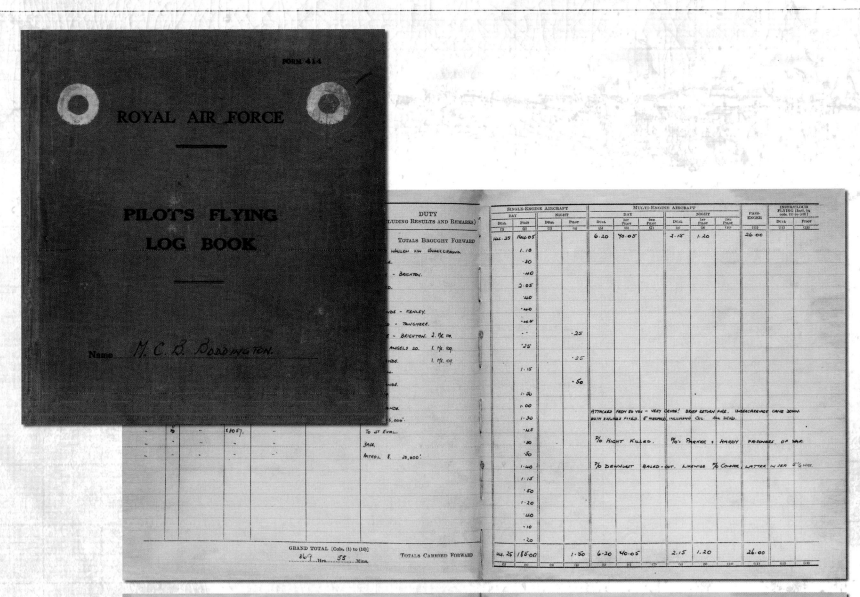

FORM 414

ROYAL AIR FORCE

PILOT'S FLYING LOG BOOK

Name **M. C. B. Boddington.**

Top log spread — Duty (Including Results and Remarks):

TOTALS BROUGHT FORWARD

- Wallon via Underground.
- — Brighton.
- — Kenley.
- — Tangmere.
- — Brighton. 2. Me. 110.
- — Angels 20. 1. Me. 109.
- — 1. Me. 109.
- To St Eval.
- Base.
- Patrol B. 20,000'.

ATTACKED FROM 50 YDS — VERY CRUDE! BRIEF RETURN FIRE. UNDERCARRIAGE CAME DOWN. BOTH ENGINES FIXED. 5" WOUND, INCLUDING OIL. MR DEAD.

P/O HIGHT KILLED. P/O's PARKER + HARDY PRISONERS OF WAR.

P/O DEWHURST BALED-OUT. LIKEWISE P/O CONNOR, LATTER IN SEA 5½ HRS.

GRAND TOTAL (Cols. (1) to (10)) ... 369 Hrs 55 Mins ... TOTALS CARRIED FORWARD

Bottom log spread:

YEAR 1940		AIRCRAFT		PILOT, OR 1ST PILOT	2ND PILOT, PUPIL OR PASSENGER	DUTY (INCLUDING RESULTS AND REMARKS)
MONTH	DATE	Type	No.			
						TOTALS BROUGHT FORWARD
AUG.	21	SPITFIRE	2289	SELF	-	SCRAMBLE.
"	24		9494			
"	25					
"	26					CRASH LANDING. SHELL IN S'BD OUTBOARD GUNS. SIMONE 1ST EXT.
"	24	MAGISTER	N3858			To St Eval.
"	28					To Middle Wallop.
"	29	SPITFIRE	F			Target.
"	30		F			Patrol Base.
"	31		F			Patrol Brooklands.
"		MAGISTER	N3858	-	SGT HORNPIPE	To St Eval.

SUMMARY FOR "B"
AUGUST FLIGHT SPITFIRE
1940 234 SQDN. MAGISTER
SIGNED .... O.C. "B" FLIGHT
SIGNED .... O.C. 234 SQDN.

GRAND TOTAL (Cols. (1) to (10)) ... 351 Hrs 15 Mins ... TOTALS CARRIED FORWARD

Cartoon (signed Brockbank):
"—'Now you let off the black smoke in both engines and let down the undercart while I dive into this cloud hopelessly out of control.'"

THE BOMBER
WAR

After the Battle of Britain and the Blitz were over, bombing offered the United Kingdom a way to strike back at Germany at a time when grappling with the Nazi war machine on the ground was not an option. Some military commanders took this further, arguing that not only were bombers irresistible, they packed such a deadly punch that they could win a war on their own. Initially, however, despite the best efforts of the crews, a lack of suitable aircraft, poor navigational and bomb-aiming equipment and inadequate training meant that the first raids were very inaccurate.

Soon, to minimize losses, the RAF switched from day to night attacks, and accuracy suffered further. In 1941, a survey reported that during this phase of the offensive, only one out of every three bombers managed to drop its bomb load within eight miles (13 kilometres) of its target.

In February 1942, the British government reappraised the role of Bomber Command. Precision attacks were deemed too difficult to carry out successfully; instead it was to focus on area bombing. The aim was to destroy the morale of the enemy populace, smash German industry and wear down their ability to make war. The morality of this decision – effectively putting German civilians in the front line of battle – was debated even at the time, and would continue to be controversial in the years that followed. The man charged with implementing this strategy

was Bomber Command's new chief, Arthur Harris, a long-time believer in the war-winning potential of bombing. He presided over enormous expansion of the effort, including development and entry into service of new heavy bombers, application of science to the campaign in the form of better navigation and bomb-aiming equipment, and improvement in crew training.

The RAF did not fight alone. From August 1942, the might of the United States Army Air Forces (USAAF) was added to the battle. Their aircraft persisted with daylight raids, attempting to hit precision targets. The crews fought bravely, relying on the defensive armament of their bombers to force the giant formations through to the target. Losses were crippling, however, and the accuracy of the USAAF attacks was not as good as had been hoped.

It was not until 1943 that the bombing campaign began to have a serious impact on Germany. In January, a combined strategy was agreed by the British and American forces. Sites of submarine and aircraft production were targeted round the clock, then German fighter defences. The industrial cities of the Ruhr were attacked and then, in late 1943, Berlin itself. By the summer of 1944, Allied bombers had helped prepare the ground for D-Day and had achieved command of the skies over Germany. Attacks on oil and transport infrastructure in particular began to cripple the German war machine. Cities in the east were also targeted, in order to support the Soviet Union's war effort. One of the most controversial attacks of the whole campaign was launched in this phase of the battle – against Dresden in February 1945. The city was devastated and about 40,000 people were killed.

OPPOSITE LEFT Wing Commander Guy Gibson (about to board the plane) and his crew board their Lancaster and prepare for the famous Dam Busters raid in May 1943. The attack on the dams of the Ruhr valley was devised by inventor Barnes Wallis. He developed a bouncing bomb to overcome the dam defences, which had to be delivered at very low level. A crack squadron (No. 617) was assembled, made up of the finest crews of Bomber Command. In May 1943 they successfully attacked and breached two of the dams, causing widespread damage. The raid gave a huge boost to British morale, but 53 out of the 133 men who took part were killed, and the Germans were quickly able to repair the damage.

OPPOSITE RIGHT The aftermath of the bombing of Dresden, Germany. On 13/14 February 1944, 796 Bomber Command Lancasters and 9 Mosquitoes raided the city, followed by 311 B-17s of the USAAF. The combination of explosives and incendiaries dropped caused firestorms, when the large number of burning buildings sucked in great draughts of oxygen, producing devastating gale-force winds to exacerbate the extreme temperatures. Many people were suffocated, adding to the numbers who were burned to death.

ABOVE Boeing B-17 Flying Fortresses of the 303rd Bomb Group, December 1944. USAAF bombers flew in "box" formations, designed to maximise the defensive fire that could be brought to bear on an attacking fighter. It was not uncommon for aircraft below to be struck and destroyed by the bombs dropping from aircraft flying at a higher altitude.

The "Heavies"
Avro Lancaster and Boeing B-17 Flying Fortress

The stalwart of the RAF's campaign was the Avro Lancaster (below), by far the most successful of the three heavy bombers in British service. It could carry more and bigger bombs than any other aircraft in the campaign, and was well loved by the crews who flew it. For the United States Army Air Forces (USAAF), the aircraft that came to symbolize the strategic bombing effort was the Boeing B-17 Flying Fortress. Packing a considerable defensive punch thanks to its 0.50-inch (12.7-mm) machine guns, it could not carry as many or as heavy bombs as the Lancaster.

ABOVE Aerial view of Hiroshima, Japan, after the detonation of the first operational atomic bomb on 6 August 1945. The weapon, dubbed "Little Boy", exploded with the force of 12.5 kilotons of TNT. In total, around 140,000 people were killed by the blast and the subsequent radiation.

Sir Arthur Harris
(1892–1984)

Harris joined the Royal Flying Corps during the First World War, and became an exponent of the idea of strategic bombing in the newly formed RAF. He took over RAF Bomber Command in February 1942, and immediately put his stamp on the force with the first "thousand bomber raid" on Cologne in May. He oversaw the huge expansion of his command, and was convinced that his aircraft could deliver overall victory in the war. Although he was hugely respected by his men, he was perceived to be extremely stubborn. Even in the last months of the war, he was very reluctant to divert his forces from the increasingly controversial area bombing campaign on to operations of more tactical importance.

Dresden came to symbolize the horror of the strategic bombing campaign after the war. Many have argued that, even in a situation of "total war", the fact that so many people were killed was morally unacceptable. It was certainly costly for the Allies too – around 80,000 bomber crewmen lost their lives. The fact remains, however, that although German industry was never completely smashed, and bombing alone did not win the war, the bombing campaign did have a serious effect on its eventual outcome. It kept about a million men and around 50,000 guns defending German cities and forced Germany to concentrate on air defence, rather than attack. Albert Speer, the German armaments minister who presided over German industrial expansion, called the campaign "the greatest lost battle on the German side".

Japan was spared the full force of a strategic bombing campaign until late in the war, primarily because of its location. But as soon as American B-29s became available, with their range of around 6,500 kilometres (4,000 miles), the USAAF began to strike at Japanese cities. By March 1945, American aircraft were dropping thousands of tonnes of incendiary bombs on cities such as Tokyo, causing huge fire storms. The raids had a significant effect on Japan's ability to continue the fight, even before atomic weapons were used on Hiroshima and Nagasaki in August. These two unfortunate cities would be forever associated with the ultimate destructive power of the bomber.

RIGHT North American P-51 Mustangs of the 375th Fighter Squadron, 361st Fighter Group over England. The Mustang, with its Rolls-Royce Merlin engine and long-range fuel tank, provided the USAAF with a fighter that could escort the bomber streams all the way to their targets in Germany. Crucially, the Mustang also boasted exceptional performance characteristics that meant it was more than a match for the German air defence fighters such as the Bf 109.

WORKING
WITH THE ARMIES

In the early stages of the war, the Luftwaffe showed how air power could play a pivotal role in battle strategy. Over the next six years, the Allies built on the ground attack techniques perfected by the German air force and employed aircraft in a host of other duties that had a direct impact on the war on the ground.

Spotting for the artillery continued to be an important job for aircraft. German forces made great use of the very manoeuvrable Fieseler Storch and the Allies found that the Taylorcraft Auster and Piper Cub were suitable for the role that had proved so useful during the First World War.

Aerial reconnaissance proved vital to the outcome of the war. Alongside signals intelligence, photographic information obtained by aircraft provided the Allies with a war-winning edge. The Luftwaffe were

initially successful at obtaining photographic reconnaissance, but as the war progressed, their effectiveness decreased. The RAF developed fast unarmed aircraft to take photographs – adapted Supermarine Spitfires and de Havilland Mosquitoes – unarmed, stripped down and relying on speed. But the real key to British success was the interpretation skills of the analysts back on the ground.

The results of photo-reconnaissance missions were used by all branches of the armed forces. The United States adopted British techniques,

ABOVE The view from a German observation aircraft, 1941–1942. Observation – be it local battlefield reconnaissance or spotting for the artillery – was an important duty for aircraft during the Second World War.

RIGHT Soviet Ilyushin Shturmovik ground attack aircraft heading into battle. The Shturmovik was extremely important to the Soviet war effort. It possessed a tough, rugged airframe and armour, and could be equipped with bombs, rockets, machine guns and cannons. Over 37,000 were built.

OPPOSITE US paratroopers jumping from their Douglas C-47 Skytrains, 1943. Troops jumped in groups or "sticks". Their parachutes were hooked up to a rail inside the aircraft by a static line; once they jumped, the cord would pull the parachutes from their packs automatically.

OVERLEAF German military vehicles destroyed by British rocket-firing Hawker Typhoons. Although the Typhoon was designed as a fighter, with its robust construction and high speed at low-level it found its true calling when used as a ground attack aircraft.

Sir Arthur Coningham
(1895–1948)

Coningham served in the army and joined the RFC in 1916, flying fighters in France. After a successful inter-war RAF career, he led a Bomber Command Group, before taking command of the Western Desert Air Force in 1941. His exceptional gifts as a leader and tactician were instrumental in creating a force which worked hand-in-hand with the army. He continued to prove his abilities in Tunisia, Sicily and Italy, and in 1944 commanded the Allied Second Tactical Air Force from D-Day to the final defeat of Germany. He was killed in an air accident three years after the end of the conflict.

developing reconnaissance versions of the P-38 Lightning and P-51 Mustang. The culmination of photo-intelligence efforts came on D-Day in June 1944: more than 4,500 photo-reconnaissance missions were flown to prepare for the launch of Operation "Overlord".

At the start of the war, the RAF was a long way behind the Luftwaffe when it came to direct battlefield support, having focused much of its efforts in the inter-war period on the idea of strategic bombing and home defence. It was not until the desert campaigns of 1941 that the RAF achieved real success in this area, when Hawker Hurricanes fitted with bombs were used to attack targets close to or on the front line. The key was the development of good air-to-ground communications systems, which allowed controllers on the ground to call in aircraft where needed. The Western Desert Air Force had a huge effect on the outcome of the key battles of 1942, and on through into Italy. Following these successes, the Allies converted the Republic P-47 and Hawker Typhoon into rugged fighter bombers, equipped with rockets and bombs. These aircraft were vital in the campaign in northern Europe, where the Second Tactical Air Force provided close air support for the advancing armies.

On the Eastern Front, the Soviet Red Army used its aircraft predominantly to assist the troops on the ground, attacking tanks, troops and communications. The IL-2 Shturmovik was the classic ground attack aircraft, so important to the success of the campaigns in the east that Marshal Joseph Stalin stated in 1941 that "The Red Army needs the Il-2 as it needs air and bread".

Germany developed the idea of "airborne warfare" based on experiments carried out by the Soviets in 1922. The idea was to drop troops by parachute or in gliders behind the lines, to cause shock and surprise or to capture an important target, then hold out until relieved by the advance of conventional troops. They were first used in Norway and the Allies soon adopted the idea. German airborne troops proved effective in the invasion of Crete in 1941 (although the high number of casualties dissuaded the German high command from using them again), and Allied operations began in North Africa in 1942, then Sicily in July 1943. In 1944, Allied paratroopers and glider-borne infantry secured the flanks on D-Day, fought in Holland and then in 1945 spearheaded the advance over the Rhine.

Transport aircraft were also vital to the success of several campaigns, most notably in the China-Burma-India theatre. The Allied 14th Army relied on air transports as they advanced through Burma and the famous "Chindits" – the troops who fought behind Japanese lines – were supplied by air. The air route into southwest China known as the "Hump" kept Chinese and US forces fighting, and there were many other operations that could only take place thanks to the flexibility offered by the transports.

Pierre Henri Clostermann
(1921–2006)

Clostermann (left) was one of the most successful ground attack pilots of the Second World War. He was born in Brazil and after being educated in Paris, obtained his private pilot's license in 1937. After the war broke out, he spent some time studying in the United States, before joining the Free French Air Force. He soon proved his abilities as a fighter pilot, flying firstly with No. 341 "Alsace" Squadron, then with No. 602, flying ground-attack missions. After an enforced break from operations, Clostermann flew the powerful RAF Tempest on missions supporting the advance across France and Germany. After the war, he worked in business and politics and even re-enlisted in the air force in 1956 to fly on operations in Algeria.

THE AIR WAR
AT SEA

With the possible exception of the submarine and torpedo, nothing did more than aviation to revolutionize war at sea. Maritime patrol aircraft kept watch over precious Atlantic convoys; carrier-launched torpedo bombers effectively ended the dominance of the battleship, and demonstrated that there were few places — and certainly no naval vessels — immune from attack.

The aircraft's ability to see over the horizon, harking back to the artillery spotting duties of the First World War, continued to be vital even in "traditional" big-gun naval actions, such as the Battle of the River Plate in 1939, when a Fairey Seafox launched by HMS *Achilles* helped the cruiser's guns target the *Graf Spee* pocket battleship. Catapult-launched seaplanes were an important addition to most large surface vessels for just this purpose. Large flying boats, with their fantastic endurance (the American PBY Catalina could stay airborne for 24 hours)

provided anti-submarine patrols, particularly helping to protect vital convoys on their way across the oceans. Land-based maritime patrol aircraft, such as the Consolidated Liberator, helped turn the tide in the pivotal Battle of the Atlantic in 1943.

Even the mightiest surface warships bristling with anti-aircraft weaponry were vulnerable to the threat from the air. The German battleship *Bismarck*, one of the most powerful vessels afloat, was crippled by a torpedo from a Fairey Swordfish biplane

from HMS *Ark Royal* in November 1940, leading to her eventual destruction. In the Mediterranean, the British effectively knocked the Italian surface fleet out of the war in 1940 when 21 Swordfish from HMS *Illustrious* severely damaged three battleships and a cruiser at Taranto harbour.

BELOW USS *Yorktown*, April 1942. This vessel was able to carry approximately 100 aircraft, measured nearly 250 metres (820 feet) in length and was one of over 120 US carriers of different sizes. Carriers were built by three of the main combatants – the United States, Britain and Japan.

Admiral Isoroku Yamamoto
(1884–1943)

Yamamoto understood the potential of naval aviation better than most. From the mid 1920s he was closely involved with carriers and aircraft. He oversaw the development of the Zero fighter, and unlike many of his rank in navies around the world, had little or no faith in battleships, being certain that the future belonged to the aircraft carrier. Although he opposed those who were calling for war, he masterminded what he saw as Japan's best hope for victory in the Pacific – a sudden, pre-emptive strike at the US fleet at Pearl Harbor. Although he never again achieved the same level of success, his abilities were respected by both the Japanese and Americans. He was killed in April 1943, when Allied intelligence revealed his whereabouts and a flight of American P-38 Lightnings were sent to shoot down his aircraft.

The Japanese high command was quick to see the potential of a surprise, carrier-launched attack on unsuspecting vessels in harbour as a way of dramatically shifting the balance of power in the Pacific away from the United States. Drawing in part on the lessons of Taranto, they planned a devastating attack on Pearl Harbor, home of the US Pacific Fleet. With highly trained pilots and well-developed weapons, the Japanese stunned the world in December 1941. For the loss of 29 aircraft, they seriously damaged or sunk 18 American vessels. As well as drawing the United States into the war, the attack demonstrated beyond all doubt the importance of carrier-borne

DRAFT No. 1   December 7, 1941.

PROPOSED MESSAGE TO THE CONGRESS

Yesterday, December 7, 1941, a date which will live in ~~world history~~ *infamy*

the United States of America was ~~simultaneously~~ *suddenly* and deliberately attacked

by naval and air forces of the Empire of Japan ~~without warning~~.

The United States was at the moment at peace with that nation and was

still in ~~continuing the~~ conversations with its Government and its Emperor looking

toward the maintenance of peace in the Pacific. Indeed, one hour after

Japanese air squadrons had commenced bombing in ~~Hawaii and the Philippines~~ *Oahu*

the Japanese Ambassador to the United States and his colleague delivered

to the Secretary of State a formal reply to a *recent American* ~~former~~ message. ~~from the~~

~~Secretary.~~ *While* This reply ~~contained a statement~~ *stated* *it seemed useless to*

that diplomatic negotiations ~~must be considered at an end,~~ *it* contained no threat ~~and no~~ hint *of* *war or* ~~an~~

armed attack.

It will be recorded that the distance ~~of Hawaii, and especially~~ of

Hawaii, from Japan makes it obvious that the attack ~~was~~ *was* deliberately

planned many days *or even weeks* ago. During the intervening time the Japanese Govern-

ment has deliberately sought to deceive the United States by false

statements and expressions of hope for continued peace.

aircraft. Luckily, the American carriers were not at Pearl Harbor on the day of the attack, and they would soon assume huge importance as the war in the Pacific began in earnest.

The Battle of the Coral Sea in May 1942 showed just how much the aircraft carrier had supplanted the battleship as the most important warship in the fleet. For the first time in history, a major battle between two large fleets of ships was fought using aircraft alone, as bombers from the USS *Yorktown* and *Lexington* exchanged blows with the Japanese carriers *Shōkaku* and *Zuikaku*. There were other ships in the fleets, but their role was peripheral. Coral Sea was followed by an even more significant battle: in June 1942, American aircraft – particularly Douglas Dauntless dive-bombers – destroyed four Japanese carriers that had been sent to win air superiority over the island of Midway. Like the Battle of the Coral Sea, Midway was fought well beyond the range of traditional guns.

The Allies went on the offensive in the Pacific, and at the heart of their efforts were the carriers and their precious aircraft. Fleets were organized around these vital ships. In 1944, in the Battle of the Philippine Sea in June, and the Battle of Leyte Gulf in October, the US Navy's aircraft once and for all asserted their dominance over the Japanese fleet, using aircraft to destroy their carriers. The employment of kamikaze tactics, when Japanese pilots used themselves and their aircraft as guided weapons, caused some considerable damage to the Allies, sinking or damaging over 300 vessels, but they could not be sustained.

Admiral Chester Nimitz
(1885–1966)

Nimitz was in overall command of the US Pacific Fleet after Pearl Harbor, and masterminded the Allied victory over the Japanese in the Pacific. It was Nimitz who gave approval for the Doolittle Raid on Tokyo, launched in April 1942 as a direct retaliation for Pearl Harbor, and he planned the Battle of Midway, the carrier action that, along with the invasion of Guadalcanal in August 1942, marked the turning point in the campaign. Like Admiral Yamamoto, he understood the importance of the aircraft carrier, and also made the best use of the intelligence material available to give him and his command the edge over a well-prepared enemy.

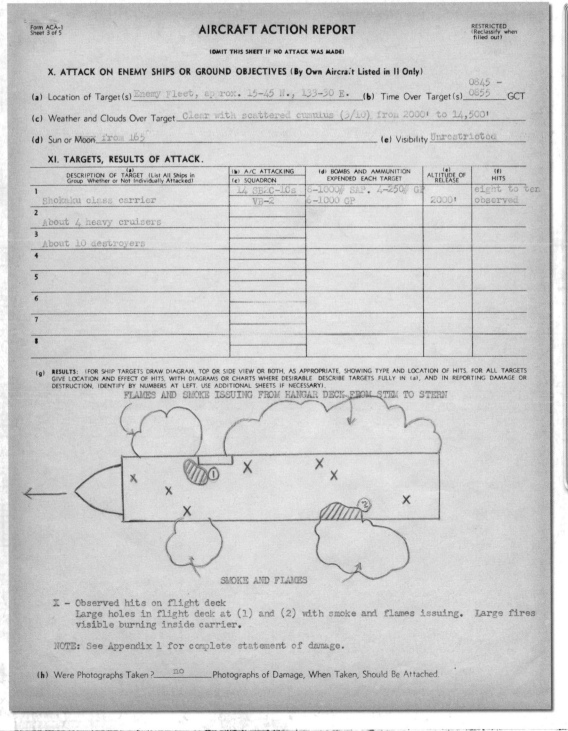

PREVIOUS PAGE A United States Navy Consolidated PB4Y-1 Liberator on an anti-submarine patrol over the Bay of Biscay. Such aircraft played a vital role in winning the Battle of Atlantic against the U-boats that threatened Allied convoys.

OPPOSITE President Franklin D Roosevelt's message to Congress after the Japanese attack on Pearl Harbor. Roosevelt went to Congress seeking its approval to declare war. The US Senate approved 82 votes to 0 and the House of Representatives voted in favour 388-1.

LEFT Aircraft Action Report from a Curtiss Helldiver squadron operating from USS *Hornet*. It describes the action of 20 June 1940 during the Battle of the Philippine Sea, when over 200 US carrier aircraft attacked a Japanese carrier group, sinking the *Hiyō*.

INDUSTRY AND
NEW TECHNOLOGIES

The Second World War forced the richest nations on earth to direct the vast majority of their industrial and scientific resources into producing military equipment. The level of achievement of the men and women in the factories and the scientists and engineers in countless design offices and laboratories was staggering. Warfare always acts as an accelerator for development, and the largest conflict in the history of mankind prompted unprecedented leaps forward. With the appearance of the jet engine and radar, rockets and nuclear weapons, no field was as affected as much as aviation.

Aircraft production by the Axis powers (Germany, Italy and Japan) was not able to match that of the Allies, a crucial reason for the ultimate outcome of the war. In 1938, Britain manufactured fewer than 3,000 military aircraft. By 1944, the UK was producing 26,000 machines annually. In the United States, the expansion was even more impressive. Fewer than 2,000 aircraft were built in American factories in 1938, but during 1944 this figure increased to over 96,000. By the end of the war, Allied aircraft were outnumbering enemy aircraft in all theatres of conflict by a ratio of at least 5 to 1. This unprecedented growth involved the use of a wide range of existing factories, the construction of many new purpose-built sites and the recruitment of thousands of women

into the plants. All of this would give aviation an enormous boost in peacetime.

It was not just the volume of production that defeated Nazi Germany. Continued technological development was key to maintaining control of the skies. In this area, Germany threatened at first to match and even surpass Allied inventions. The Nazi regime invested a great deal of money and effort in experimental projects which they hoped would produce a "wonder weapon" that could win the war. Although incredible advances were made (for example, rocket engines), they came too late to have any effect on the eventual outcome of the conflict. But the German research was to prove vital to the future post-war development of space rockets, missiles

RIGHT The VS-300, created by Igor Sikorsky, became the first successful helicopter after its historic tethered flight on September 14, 1939. The following spring, the helicopter could stay airborne for as long as 15 minutes, and in 1941 it established a world record world a flight of 1 hour, 32 minutes, and 26 seconds.

Igor Sikorsky
(1889–1972)

Sikorsky was born in Kiev. Throughout his childhood he was fascinated by aviation, particularly the concept of a helicopter. In 1913, he designed and built giant four-engine aeroplanes – the first such machines ever to fly. He became famous for his 2,600-kilometre (1,600-mile) flight from St Petersburg to Kiev in 1914 in the four-engined *Il'ya Muromets*. After moving to America to escape the revolution, Sikorsky built flying boats before turning his attention once again to helicopters. His breakthrough idea was to position a small vertical rotor on the tail to counteract the torque of the main rotor. This configuration can be seen on most modern helicopters.

and record-breaking aircraft (such as the formidable sound-barrier-smashing Bell X-1, flown by Chuck Yeager in 1947).

The jet engine was born simultaneously in Britain and Germany in the 1930s. In the United Kingdom, Frank Whittle developed the turbojet that would go on to power the Gloster Meteor. In Germany, it was Hans von Ohain whose work led to the creation of a functioning turbojet. Following Germany's defeat, it was left to Britain to lead the world in this exciting new technology. Soon however, America and the Soviet Union began making great strides forwards in jet engine development. Other European designers rapidly caught up, most notably the French with the jet-powered Dassault Ouragan fighter.

Radar had an enormous impact on aviation. In 1935, Robert Watson-Watt led the research in Britain that created the radio-wave device that could detect aircraft at great range. Parallel research was being conducted in Germany too, leading to similar systems. Radar would form the basis of many of the technologies that were vital to the development of aviation in the second half of the twentieth century, including military weapons systems and civil air traffic control.

Helicopters first entered service in the Second World War, but the compromise between the helicopter and fixed wing aircraft, the autogyro, was originally pioneered in the 1930s. Many engineers around the world worked on true vertical take-off machines, including Louis Breguet of France and the German, Heinrich Focke. However, the man most associated with the genesis of the helicopter is Igor Sikorsky, whose VS-300 led to the world's first production helicopter, the R-4 Hoverfly, used by the Allies in significant numbers after 1942.

The creation and use of the atomic bomb would shape the future of aviation as much as any other technology. Aircraft were tasked with delivering these devastating weapons, and the Cold War was defined by their ability to drop them on cities thousands of kilometres away.

OPPOSITE Women work on the production line of Hawker Hurricanes. By 1943 over seven million British women were in paid work, carrying out many of the "home front" duties that had once been the preserve of men.

BELOW Sir Frank Whittle (1907–1996), right, pioneer of the jet engine, explains the workings of a turbojet. Whittle joined the RAF in 1923 as an engineer apprentice, before becoming a pilot and an officer. His initial idea for a turbojet was rejected by the Air Ministry, but with the backing of the RAF, Whittle continued his engineering studies, subsequently founding the company Power Jets in 1936 in order to develop his designs.

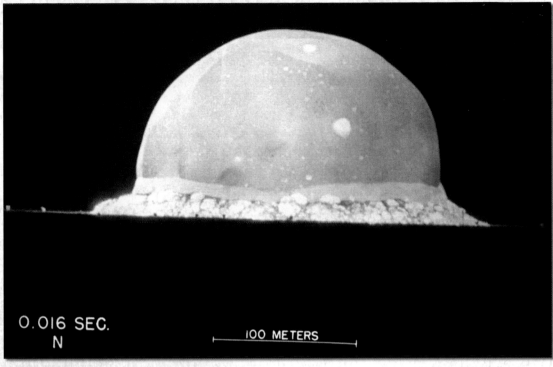

ABOVE The first atomic bomb test was carried out in New Mexico, USA, on 16 July 1945. It was developed by a team of scientists under the direction of J Robert Oppenheimer. The project was codenamed "Manhattan".

LEFT Consolidated B-24 bombers at Henry Ford's Willow Run plant, February 1943. The United States' industrial might far outstripped that of any other nation. The Willow Run factory alone was 1.6 kilometres (0.9 miles) long and nearly 400 metres (1,312 feet) wide, and produced over 8,500 aircraft. By the middle of 1945 the US aviation industry was using nearly 15 million square metres (161 million square feet) of space across the country.

Marcel Dassault
(1892–1986)

Born Marcel Bloch, Dassault changed his name after the Second World War. Dassault had been the wartime resistance codename of his brother Paul. Before the Second World War, Bloch had been involved in the design of several military and civil aircraft and after 1940 he joined the resistance. He was captured in 1944 and imprisoned in Buchenwald concentration camp. After the war, Dassault spearheaded the design of many outstanding aircraft, including the *Mystère* and the *Mirage*. He is widely regarded as responsible for the growth and success of the post-war French aircraft industry.

AIR TRAVEL
IN THE POST WAR WORLD

Before the Second World War, air travel was a growing but hardly practical alternative to traditional forms of transport. After it, air travel began to shrink the world. This was caused by several factors. Great technological strides were made in aircraft development, including sophisticated navigation and communications equipment. The war created a large group of people around the world very familiar with aircraft and aviation — including thousands of ex-military aircrew and ground crew — and a network of former wartime airfields was scattered all over the globe, ready to be converted into airports. Particularly in the United States, the massive industrial effort that had produced over 300,000 combat aircraft could easily be switched to manufacturing commercial aircraft. Where this was not possible, there were military transport designs that could be easily converted, as happened in Britain.

International agreement was needed to control all of this. The 1944 Chicago Convention, at which over 50 nations were represented, updated the many bilateral agreements that had previously governed international flight. While it did not completely open up the skies, it did set a framework that allowed air travel to expand and develop. The International Air Transport Association (IATA), established in 1949, governed international air routes and regulated what could and could not be charged for flights. Most airlines were heavily subsidized or owned by their national governments – so-called "national carriers".

In the United States, undoubtedly the world leader in civil aviation, the government saw to it that competition between the major airlines was controlled. Pan American, American Overseas Airways, Transcontinental and Western Airlines (TWA – which after

RIGHT Baggage is loaded into a British Overseas Airways Corporation (BOAC) Avro Lancastrian airliner in the 1940s. The Lancastrian is an example of an ex-military aircraft being successfully adapted for civilian use, based as it was on the Avro Lancaster bomber. It served on several routes, including Britain to Australia, and the type carried both passengers and mail.

OPPOSITE The Boeing Stratocruiser Flying Cloud at Heathrow, London, April 1949, after completing its first transatlantic flight. The Stratocruiser was purposely named to reflect the fact that with its pressured cabin, it could cruise in the stratosphere, above any turbulent weather. It was essentially a newly designed double-deck fuselage with the wings and tail of a B-29 bomber.

The Lockheed Constellation series

Constellations are widely regarded as some of the most beautiful airliners ever built. Designed by Clarence "Kelly" Johnson, the first variant in the series, the L-049, was requisitioned for military transport use during the Second World War and designated the C-69. After the war the design was developed further into the ultimate version, the L-1049 Super-Constellation. Constellations were operated by several airlines, the most famous being TWA, and their pressurized cabins and long range made them popular with passengers.

In Flight with TWA . . .

TWA'S Super-Constellation SKYLINER

You enjoy luxury living aloft as you fly smoothly in TWA's dependable, giant new Super-Constellation Skyliners, the latest word in swift, modern passenger aircraft.

TWA
TRANS WORLD AIRLINES
U.S.A. · EUROPE
AFRICA · ASIA

Donald Douglas
(1892–1981)

Donald Douglas established the Douglas aircraft manufacturing company – one of the most prestigious names in aviation, responsible for some of the most successful aircraft ever built. He studied at the Massachusetts Institute of Technology, and then began his career at Martin aircraft before founding the Douglas Aircraft Company in 1921. Following the Second World War, he was responsible for creating the DC series of aircraft, including the legendary DC-3. After the war, Douglas continued to play a key role in the development of passenger flight, developing the DC-6 and DC-7.

OPPOSITE A Douglas DC-7C of Dutch airline KLM. The DC-7, the final variant of the four piston-engine DC series, could carry just over 100 passengers at a cruising speed of 580 kilometres per hour (360 miles per hour).

BELOW A BOAC steward serving a passenger on a Bristol Britannia in the mid 1950s. The promise of high-quality food and well-prepared meals was often used to entice customers, especially at a time when ticket prices were set by the IATA and cost could not be used to undercut the competition.

A really royal welcome...

AWAITS YOU ABOARD THE MONARCH

ELEGANCE, LUXURY and impeccable service... these are the keynotes when you travel by *The Monarch*, the B.O.A.C. *de luxe* service between London and New York. You fly overnight smoothly above the weather in a pressurized and air-conditioned Stratocruiser. This magnificent, double-decked airliner, with tasteful decor, restful lighting and luxurious dressing rooms, is so spacious it seems like a flying hotel. You relax —really relax—in the superb comfort of a foam-soft armchair; then, for a change of scene, you have only to walk down the spiral staircase to find yourself in the sociable, club-like atmosphere of the large bar-lounge on the lower deck. Not the least of your enjoyments are the meals, served on individual tables. The *cuisine* on board *The Monarch* is given extra special attention—every dish is designed for the palate of the connoisseur. A seven-course dinner, prefaced by cocktails, is served with wines, including champagne, and rounded off by a choice of liqueurs—all with the compliments of B.O.A.C.

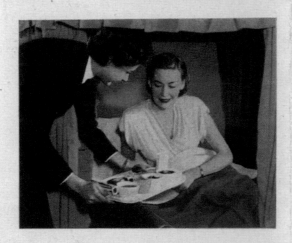

Three stewards and a stewardess attend to your every wish in the traditional English way—with courtesy, efficiency and friendliness. For a small additional charge, you may enjoy a perfect night's rest in a full-length sleeping berth—awaking, of course, to the delight of breakfast in bed. When you travel by *The Monarch*, you reap the benefits of B.O.A.C.'s 34 years' experience in airline operation—the highest possible standards of operational efficiency and every conceivable improvement which can be devised for your pleasure and comfort. To fly *Monarch* is to enjoy the gay atmosphere of transatlantic air travel at its best—yet you pay no extra to travel by this luxurious service!

1950 stood for Trans World Airlines, reflecting its enhanced global role) all lobbied the US government to win the right to conduct transatlantic flights to Europe.

The magnificent piston-engine aircraft that flew these routes were made by giant manufacturers who had been responsible for some of the finest combat aircraft of the Second World War – in particular Lockheed and McDonnell Douglas. The Lockheed Constellation – affectionately known as the "Connie" – is still widely regarded as a design classic, instantly recognizable with its triple tail. Matching the successive generations of Connies, Super Constellations and Starliners were the Douglas-built DC-6s and DC-7s, together with the Boeing Stratocruiser.

Although passenger travel was growing rapidly, it was by no means open to all. Prices were set high, barring most from the experience. Airlines sought to compete by offering still more luxurious services, with comfortable cabins and better food, replicating – and in many ways surpassing – the services offered in the age of the pre-war flying boats. Advances in engine technology and cabin pressurization meant that turbulence and poor weather could be more easily avoided, and journey times were considerably shortened. But, although in the 1950s piston-engine aircraft provided reliable flights across the oceans and the vast continent of the United States, there was a limit to how far the piston engine could be pushed.

Jet technology, which had been developed during the Second World War and used to power combat aircraft, was slow to be adapted to civil aviation. Jet engines were expensive to run and could not offer the same reliability as the tried-and-tested piston designs. Britain led the way in developing jet technology, first using it in a civil context with the turboprop – using the power of the jet engine to drive a propeller as well as the turbine. Turboprop airliners, such as the British Vickers Viscount, which entered airline service in 1950, bridged the gap between the piston engine and the jet age – when civil aviation truly began to open up for all.

LEFT A publicity leaflet produced by BOAC advertising their London–New York luxury "Monarch" passenger service. This was introduced in March 1951 using the Boeing Stratocruiser. Highlights included a seven-course meal, cocktails and sleeping berths.

COLD WAR
CONFRONTATION

The dropping of atomic weapons on Japan in 1945 ushered in the nuclear age. The post-war confrontation between the Soviet Union and the West was based on the threat of Mutually Assured Destruction (the military doctrine that the side which launched a nuclear attack itself risked certain and total destruction in a counter-strike), and aircraft were at the forefront of the stand-off. Given the often vast distances involved, aircraft remained for many years the best way of delivering nuclear payloads. Airpower was vital in other ways too: U2 and SR-71 spy planes watched over enemy territory, and interceptor fighters stood poised to shoot the bombers down, while transports kept the beleaguered city of Berlin supplied in 1948 and 1949.

Berlin was an obvious flashpoint during the Cold War, situated deep in Soviet-controlled East Germany and itself divided between the victorious Allies. When the Soviet Union decided to block the land routes to the Western sector of the city, and so effectively starve the Western Allies out, the only way to keep Berlin alive was to supply it by air. Thus began the largest air supply operation ever mounted. Over a ten-month period, transports, mainly from the RAF and USAF, made around 277,000 flights. Half a decade earlier, many of the pilots had been delivering deadly cargoes of bombs to Berlin – now they brought food, coal and other essential supplies, which forced the Soviets to end the blockade in May 1949.

Throughout the 1950s, the focus for both sides was making sure that the nuclear deterrent was a realistic and effective one. Each had to convince the other that it had the will to use, and the capability to deliver, nuclear weapons. For America in particular, this meant building vast bomber fleets. In 1947, the USAF possessed just ten B-29s. Over the next ten years, a series of bombers were developed – including the Boeing B-47 and giant Convair B-36 – culminating in the B-52, one of the longest-serving aircraft ever built. In the United Kingdom, the nuclear deterrent was carried by the V-bombers – the Valiant, Victor and Vulcan. Soviet efforts produced the Tupolev Tu-95 in 1956, a turboprop-powered bomber with greater range than its predecessors.

OPPOSITE A USAF C-54 Skymaster delivers its cargo to Berlin during the airlift. The C-54 was just one of the types that kept the city supplied. Others included USAF C-47 Skytrains and C-74 Globemasters, RAF Short Sunderlands, Avro Yorks and Handley Page Hastings.

Clarence "Kelly" Johnson
(1910–1990)

Johnson was one of the most innovative and creative aircraft designers in American history. He began working for Lockheed in 1933, and as the company's chief engineer designed several famous aircraft, including the P-38 Lightning and the Constellation passenger aeroplane. During the Second World War he developed the P-80 jet fighter, and the unit he assembled for that job – known as the "Skunk Works" after a 1940s comic strip – was a model of productive efficiency. The team applied their considerable talents to the development of the F-104 Starfighter, the U2 and SR-71 reconnaissance aircraft – all stalwarts of the Cold War.

Major Rudolf Anderson
(1927–1962)

Anderson was part of Strategic Air Command's 4080th Strategic Reconnaissance Wing, which provided key intelligence on the build up of Soviet missiles in Cuba. Anderson and Major Richard S Heyser made several flights over Cuba, bringing back photographs that helped President John F Kennedy to negotiate their removal with Soviet leader Nikita Krushchev. Then, on 27 October 1962, Anderson was killed when his aircraft was shot down by an SA-2 Surface-to-Air Missile. Anderson was the only American killed by enemy fire during the Cuban missile crisis.

Intelligence gathering was a vital part of military strategy. The American company Lockheed produced two of the most iconic spy planes of the war – the U2 and the SR-71 Blackbird. Spy flights did not always go to plan – an international incident was caused when a U2 was shot down in 1960 over the Soviet Union and its pilot, Gary Powers, was captured. But the information the U2s provided was invaluable. Missions over Cuba obtained vital intelligence on the build-up of Soviet missiles during the Cuban missile crisis.

Defence against nuclear bombers was the job of interceptor fighters. Speed was the key here, and the aircraft designed in the 1950s to do this job were missile-carrying jet fighters with extremely powerful engines. Aircraft such as the American Convair F-106 and the British English Electric Lightning typified this approach. In addition to fighter defence, Surface-to-Air Missiles (SAMs) formed a vital part of anti-aircraft systems. Some believed that the SAM would wholly replace the manned fighter, and they proved very effective at shooting down high-level aircraft, such as spy planes.

Missiles were not employed just to bring down aircraft. From the early 1960s, when technology had overcome many of the disadvantages of unmanned systems, and the missiles became fitted with nuclear payloads, they began to replace the bomber. Both Intercontinental Ballistic Missiles (ICBMs) and submarine-launched systems such as Polaris had distinct advantages over bombers. Missile silos were easier to hide than airfields, and submarines found it easier still to remain undetected. Ballistic missiles were largely impervious to being shot down, either by fighters or missiles. And, perhaps most importantly, they were very much faster than bombers, shortening the time the enemy would have to launch a counter-strike before being annihilated by the overwhelming power of a nuclear attack.

LEFT Test-firing a US LGM-30 Minuteman Intercontinental Ballistic Missile. The first Minuteman entered service in the early 1960s. The current variant, Minuteman III, is capable of traveling at 24,000 kilometres per hour (nearly 15,000 mile per hour), with a range of around 10,000 kilometres (6,200 miles).

OVERLEAF A large crowd of anti-nuclear weapons protesters from the CND (Campaign for Nuclear Disarmament) in Trafalgar Square, London, 1959. The overwhelming destructive power of nuclear weapons led many people to join disarmament groups. In the UK, protests were often held against the nuclear weapons – first bombs, then missiles – based in Britain as part of the country's commitment to NATO.

AIR POWER
IN KOREA AND VIETNAM

Half a decade after the end of the Second World War and less than a year after the Berlin Airlift, East and West again clashed when Communist North Korea invaded its southern neighbour in 1950. Barely a decade after that, the United States was again at war in Asia, this time attempting to prevent a Communist takeover of South Vietnam. Although these conflicts were brutal and protracted, both stopped short of all-out nuclear war. Rather than delivering knock-out strategic nuclear blows, aircraft in Korea and Vietnam carried out the same jobs that they had undertaken in the First and Second World Wars: conventional bombing, fighting for superiority in the air over the battlefield and, most importantly, supporting soldiers on the ground.

Aircraft immediately proved their worth in the earliest phases of the Korean War, halting and repelling the Communist advance through tactical bombing. The aircraft that carried out these ground-attack missions were mainly older types dating back to the Second World War, such as the American B-29 Superfortress and P-51 Mustang. These machines again proved how aircraft could be used to alter the course of a battle. When China entered the conflict, with its high-performance MiG-15 fighters, US aerial dominance over the battlefield was put in jeopardy. The USAF then introduced its own next-generation aircraft – notably the F-86 Sabre – which meant that for the first time, jets fought jets.

The role of the aircraft as military transport was dramatically demonstrated in Korea, particularly in the early stage of the conflict, which was characterized by rapid advance and equally rapid withdrawal. Cargo aircraft delivered supplies and airlifted troops, as well as providing a vital air bridge with US bases in Japan. And for the first time helicopters played a significant part in a campaign, particularly in the transport role, and especially in evacuating casualties.

By the mid 1960s, America had become involved in another "hot war" against communism, this time in Vietnam. The USAF was the most powerful air force in the world, yet in a decade of fighting, it was unable to translate that overwhelming might into victory on the battlefield. In March 1965, Operation "Rolling Thunder" was launched, a bombing campaign targeted against North Vietnam. It was hoped that this would force the Communists to give up, but it proved unsuccessful. Similar campaigns later in the war were similarly unsuccessful. The detailed rules of engagement that forced the USAF to avoid many targets and the resilience of the enemy were just two of the reasons that prevented the bomber having a decisive impact on the war.

Helicopters – epitomized by the Bell UH-1 Huey – were the true workhorses of the Vietnam War, expanding upon the role that they fulfilled in Korea. They ferried troops into action, evacuated casualties and undertook ground-attack missions with rockets and machine guns. Close air support was also provided by fixed-wing aircraft such as the piston-engined A-1 Skyraider and the jet F-4 Phantom. The fighters did not enjoy the same degree of success in aerial combat as they had in Korea, partly because of the strict rules of engagement – US pilots had to have visual confirmation of enemy aircraft, negating any advantage they may have had from their air-to-air missiles.

RIGHT The North American F-86 Sabre. The battles that took place between the USAF F-86s and the Communist MiG-15s were fought using machine guns and cannons, and the tactics used were similar to those employed in the Second World War. The crucial difference was that the faster speed at which the jet fighters flew meant that more airspace was needed for dogfights.

Air power did not win the Vietnam War. Whether fighting against US jet fighters or helicopter-borne "aerial cavalry", the enemy found ways to avoid combat on anything but the most favourable terms. Ultimately, the most significant advances to come out the conflict were technological, not tactical or strategic. These included "smart" weapons, electronic warfare and advanced anti-aircraft systems, all of which would be refined and used in later conflicts.

OPPOSITE Men of the United States 1st Air Cavalry about to board their helicopter. The US "airmobile" tactics were designed to cope with the varied terrain of Vietnam and the elusiveness of the enemy forces. Troops could be quickly moved into battle and supported from the air.

LEFT A USAF P-51 Mustang releasing napalm over North Korea in 1951. The piston engine P-51 was a Second World War design that proved to be very successful in the ground-attack role. However, piston-engine fighters could not hope to match the air-to-air combat ability of the jet fighters which began to be used as the war progressed.

OVERLEAF A US Navy F4-B Phantom attacks a Viet Cong position. Ground troops would often call on aircraft to provide close air support against well-concealed guerrilla forces.

Lieutenant-Colonel Vermont Garrison (1915–1994)

Vermont Garrison was the oldest of the Korean War "aces", eventually shooting down 10 MiGs. Like many of the Korean War pilots, Garrison was also a very successful Second World War fighter pilot. The "aces" of the Korean War attracted much public attention. Competition was fierce between the Sabre pilots to record the most "kills", just as it had been in previous conflicts, particularly in the First World War. The Sabres were often outnumbered by the MiGs, who also fought much closer to their bases. But the USAF pilots were better trained and crucially much more experienced.

Boeing B-52 Stratofortress

The B-52 was the ultimate Cold War weapon, designed to deliver nuclear bombs on to Soviet cities. So successful was the design that B-52s remain in service today, and for the foreseeable future. The B-52 was dramatically re-purposed during the Vietnam War, being used to drop 225- or 340-kilogram- (500- or 750-pound-) bombs on tactical targets such as enemy supply routes or camps, or in support of ground forces. The use of such overwhelming force (essentially carpet-bombing) was justified at the time because of the difficulty in spotting pinpoint targets in the dense jungle. But after the war, the proportionality of the raids was questioned, given the huge tonnage of bombs dropped for little real gain.

BELOW A USAF Boeing B-52 drops its bombs. Despite being developed as a strategic bomber, during the Vietnam War B-52s were often used to carpet-bomb areas of jungle in order to knock out supply routes, troops and camps. In the process they destroyed several square kilometres of jungle or rice paddy field at a time.

THE SPACE
RACE

Space flight in the 1960s was made possible thanks to technological advances during the Second World War, while the enormous developments that were required to send people first into orbit, and then to the Moon, would not have happened as rapidly without the near-fatal clash of ideologies that formed the Cold War.

It had been considered that only the explosive power of the rocket engine could reliably overcome the Earth's gravity. In the 1930s, it was Germany that led the field in this research. The Nazi regime invested a great deal of money and effort into developing rockets as weapons, culminating in the creation of the V2. This was designed by the best German scientists available led by the brilliant Wernher von Braun, and built by slave labour and prisoners of war.

As they advanced across Germany, the Americans and Soviets rushed to secure the expertise of the engineers responsible for the V2s. Von Braun and over 100 of his colleagues were spirited to the United States. Others – mainly lower ranking scientists than those in von Braun's team – ended up in Russia, enhancing a rocket programme that had been second only to Germany's in the 1920s and 1930s. By the 1950s, under the

OPPOSITE The *Saturn V* rocket designed to launch the Apollo missions to the moon. 15 *Saturn Vs* were built. They were over 100 metres (330 feet) tall and propelled by a combination of kerosene, liquid oxygen and liquid nitrogen, powering a total of 11 engines: five in the first stage, five in the second and one in the third.

BELOW The seven astronauts selected for Project Mercury were all highly skilled military test-pilots who met very stringent standards of physical fitness. The Mercury astronauts were Alan Shephard, M Scott Carpenter, John Glenn, Donald "Deke" Slayton, Virgil "Gus" Grissom, Wally Schirra and L Gordon Cooper.

gifted Sergei Korolev, the Soviet Union had already developed rockets that could generate more than twice as much thrust as their American counterparts.

The Soviets achieved the first significant advances with the launch of their *Sputnik* satellite in October 1957. They made a great show of their successes, which in turn fuelled America's desire not to be seen as technologically inferior to the Communists. The US responded with the launch of the satellite *Explorer I* in January 1958. What subsequently became known as the "Space Race" had begun in earnest.

Next on the list of notable firsts was manned space flight. Again, the Soviet Union beat the American efforts by launching "Cosmonaut" Yuri Gagarin on an orbital flight in April 1961. "Astronaut" Alan Shephard became the first American in space in May of the same year, and later the same month

President Kennedy announced that it would be the goal of the United States to put a man on the Moon and return him safely to Earth by the end of the decade. Determined to maintain their lead, the Soviets also attempted to reach the prize. The American National Aeronautics and Space Administration (NASA) worked methodically through the considerable problems of directing a crew to a target 400,000 kilometres (250,000 miles) away. Astronauts were launched on ever more advanced and demanding missions that culminated in July 1969 with Apollo 11, which landed Neil Armstrong and Edwin "Buzz" Aldrin on the Moon.

Both the American public and politicians began to lose interest in the Apollo programme after the first few missions, and on 14 December 1972 astronaut Gene Cernan became the last person to walk on the Moon. The Soviet space programme had by now

LEFT The International Space Station. Many nations have contributed elements to the project, principally the United States and Russia. It consists of several distinct modules, each fulfilling a different function. These include crew quarters and laboratory facilities. Components are carried into orbit by shuttles or rockets.

Werner von Braun
(1912–1977)

Von Braun was the most important scientist in the German pre-war investigations into rocketry. He maintained after the war that his work on weapons was a means to an end, and that his real interest and passion was for manned space travel. At the end of the war he was determined to offer his services to the Americans, rather than the Soviets, and he became the leading figure in the development of American rockets – both the deadly ICBMs and the more benign space vehicles.

MSC-00171

APOLLO 11 MISSION REPORT

PREPARED BY

Mission Evaluation Team

APPROVED BY

George M. Low
Manager, Apollo Spacecraft Program

NATIONAL AERONAUTICS AND SPACE ADMINISTRATION
MANNED SPACECRAFT CENTER
HOUSTON, TEXAS
November 1969

1.0 SUMMARY

The purpose of the Apollo 11 mission was to land men on the lunar surface and to return them safely to earth. The crew were Neil A. Armstrong, Commander; Michael Collins, Command Module Pilot; and Edwin E. Aldrin, Jr., Lunar Module Pilot.

The space vehicle was launched from Kennedy Space Center, Florida, at 8:32:00 a.m., e.s.t., July 16, 1969. The activities during earth orbit checkout, translunar injection, transposition and docking, spacecraft ejection, and translunar coast were similar to those of Apollo 10. Only one midcourse correction, performed at about 27 hours elapsed time, was required during translunar coast.

The spacecraft was inserted into lunar orbit at about 76 hours, and the circularization maneuver was performed two revolutions later. Initial checkout of lunar module systems was satisfactory, and after a planned rest period, the Commander and Lunar Module Pilot entered the lunar module to prepare for descent.

The two spacecraft were undocked at about 100 hours, followed by separation of the command and service modules from the lunar module. Descent orbit insertion was performed at approximately 101-1/2 hours, and powered descent to the lunar surface began about 1 hour later. Operation of the guidance and descent propulsion systems was nominal. The lunar module was maneuvered manually approximately 1100 feet downrange from the nominal landing point during the final 2-1/2 minutes of descent. The spacecraft landed in the Sea of Tranquillity at 102:45:40. The landing coordinates were 0 degrees 41 minutes 15 seconds north latitude and 23 degrees 26 minutes east longitude referenced to lunar map ORB-II-6(100), first edition, December 1967. During the first 2 hours on the surface, the two crewmen performed a postlanding checkout of all lunar module systems. Afterwards, they ate their first meal on the moon and elected to perform the surface operations earlier than planned.

Considerable time was deliberately devoted to checkout and donning of the back-mounted portable life support and oxygen purge systems. The Commander egressed through the forward hatch and deployed an equipment module in the descent stage. A camera in this module provided live television coverage of the Commander descending the ladder to the surface, with first contact made at 109:24:15 (9:56:15 p.m. e.s.t., July 20, 1969). The Lunar Module Pilot egressed soon thereafter, and both crewmen used the initial period on the surface to become acclimated to the reduced gravity and unfamiliar surface conditions. A contingency sample was taken from the surface, and the television camera was deployed so that most of the lunar module was included in its view field. The crew activated the scientific experiments, which included a solar wind detector, a passive already shifted to the potential for scientific study afforded by building space stations in orbit around the Earth – developing their technology with the *Salyut* programme, followed by the famous *Mir*. America launched *Skylab* in 1973. New levels of international co-operation were achieved by beginning the construction of the International Space Station in 1998.

While the Soviets continued to focus on rockets to launch their cosmonauts, NASA turned its attention to reusable systems which would, it was hoped, reduce the crippling level of expenditure associated with the space programme. The result was the Space Shuttle, which regrettably was not as economical as had been forecast. Intended to make space travel more routine, the programme is unfortunately remembered by many for the tragic loss of the shuttles *Challenger* in 1986 and *Columbia* in 2003. Meanwhile, in a bid to find more money for their programme, Russia began to open up space travel to the super rich.

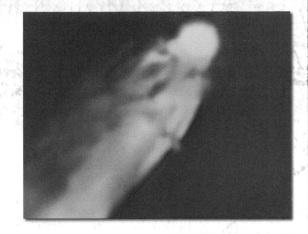

ABOVE The space shuttle *Challenger*, which exploded on 28 January 1986 with the loss of all seven crew. This dealt a severe blow to the US space programme, and shuttles did not fly again until September 1988. Seven further shuttle astronauts were lost in 2003 when *Columbia* broke up as it returned to Earth, leaving three shuttles – *Discovery*, *Endeavour* and *Atlantis* – of the original five.

LEFT AND OPPOSITE The Apollo 11 mission report. In understated detail, it describes the mission undertaken by the three-man crew, Neil Armstrong, Edwin "Buzz" Aldrin and Michael Collins. Their goal was simply summarized as "perform a manned lunar landing and return safely to Earth".

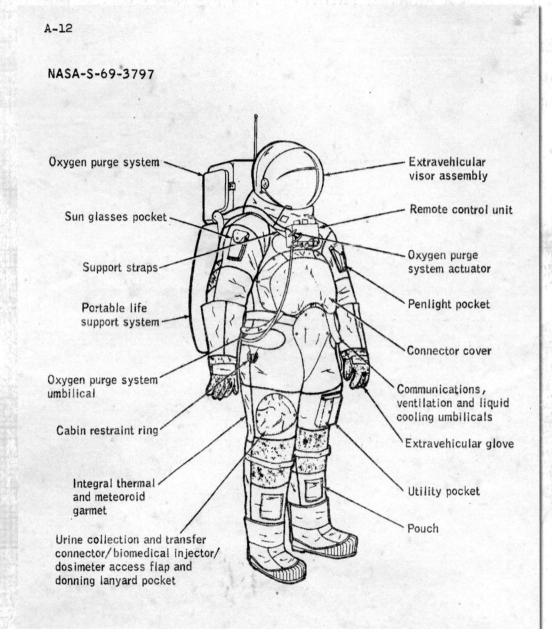

A-12

NASA-S-69-3797

Oxygen purge system

Sun glasses pocket

Support straps

Portable life support system

Oxygen purge system umbilical

Cabin restraint ring

Integral thermal and meteoroid garmet

Urine collection and transfer connector/biomedical injector/ dosimeter access flap and donning lanyard pocket

Extravehicular visor assembly

Remote control unit

Oxygen purge system actuator

Penlight pocket

Connector cover

Communications, ventilation and liquid cooling umbilicals

Extravehicular glove

Utility pocket

Pouch

Figure A-1.- Extravehicular mobility unit.

Sergei Korolev
(1906–1966)

Korolev was a qualified aeronautical engineer who was a founder member of the Moscow Group for Study of Reaction Motion in the 1930s. He led the Soviet Union's pre-war rocket research, but was arrested in 1938 as part of a Stalinist purge, charged with treason and sent to the Gulag. He was saved by being recalled to work in the Russian aircraft industry, and released in 1944. He then led the development of Soviet rockets, presiding over the most successful period in the space programme, beating the United States to several "firsts".

THE JET AGE

The jet engine revolutionized air transport. In the space of three decades, flying went from an elite form of travel to an everyday occurrence familiar to millions. Britain took the lead in jet-powered passenger aircraft with the de Havilland Comet, which entered service in 1952. The wealthy passengers that made up the majority of airline customers loved its speed, comfort and style. However, the Comet's promising career was effectively destroyed by three tragic crashes. The type was grounded while investigators discovered the problem (metal fatigue exacerbated by the aircraft's rectangular windows), and by the time the redesigned Comet 4 entered service, other companies had followed de Havilland's example and entered the jet airliner market.

This was particularly true in the United States, where Boeing led the field. In 1958, they introduced the 707, which could carry more than double the number of passengers of the re-introduced Comet 4. They were hugely popular and the Douglas Aircraft Company attempted to match Boeing's success with the larger DC-8. Although these models both served in large numbers, 707s outsold DC-8s, firmly placing Boeing in front. As technology improved and jets became more efficient and reliable, they even began to replace turboprop airliners on shorter journeys. A notable aircraft in this class was the French Sud Aviation

OPPOSITE Female flight attendants, popularly known as air hostesses (seen here in front of a de Havilland Comet), were a key part of the marketing campaigns of many airlines, particularly during the 1960s and 1970s.

BELOW Boeing 707s at the Boeing plant in Renton Washington, 1958. Although the de Havilland Comet was the first jet to operate a transatlantic service, it was soon followed by the 707 (flown by Pan Am), with flights between New York and Paris.

Boeing 747

The 747 was developed by Boeing but its expensive $2 billion development costs could only be borne thanks to a $500,000,000 advance order for 25 of the new jets by Pan Am. It proved to be a winning idea. The design was not revolutionary, but it was a very daring decision to build such a giant machine (over 70-metres- [230-feet-] long with a wingspan of nearly 60 metres [195 feet]) at a time when many felt that supersonic travel would be the next "big thing". It also meant that many airports had to be extensively modified to cope with its size. Since it first flew in 1969, the 747 has served with airlines all over the world. It has been adapted to carry freight as well as passengers, and it is one of the most recognizable aircraft ever built.

Caravelle, a medium range jet airliner that was introduced on US internal routes.

During the 1960s, Boeing developed the 727 and 737, which both proved popular with airlines. Other manufacturers created some notable designs, such as the Douglas DC-9 and the British Aircraft Corporation One-Eleven. A new aura of glamour surrounded these comfortable jets, profoundly of its time and firmly a part of 60s popular culture, and a new term – "the jet set" – was coined to describe the flyers who enjoyed the globe trotting lifestyle. Passenger numbers began to increase, especially in the United Kingdom, thanks to the continued expansion of "package tours", when single tour operators sold whole holidays, including air travel and accommodation, at discounted prices.

The obvious next step for passenger travel was increased speed, specifically the breaking of the sound barrier. In the US, Boeing began developing the 2707. In the Soviet Union, Tupolev designed the Tu-144. But only one supersonic design made it from drawing board to successful airline service; the Anglo-French BAC/Aérospatiale Concorde, which first flew in 1969 – around a decade after all of the programmes began. It proved very difficult to get clearance to operate what was felt by some to be an extremely noisy, fuel hungry, ecologically unsound aircraft – especially in the United States, and the only way to offset the enormous development and operating costs was to charge astronomical prices for tickets, meaning that few could afford the luxury. Concorde proved to be too expensive for most passengers' pockets and, although it was very popular with the minority who could afford the experience, it was only ever operated by two airlines.

The future turned out not to belong to the fastest, but to the biggest. At the same time as Concorde was being designed and built, Boeing developed the 747 (popularly known as the "Jumbo"), able to carry over 400 passengers. Nothing as big had been built before; fewer than 200 passengers was the norm. The 747 was followed by the McDonnell Douglas DC-10 and the Lockheed TriStar. However, the difficult world economic conditions meant that the airline industry found it hard to prosper in the 1970s, despite the introduction of these so-called "wide bodies".

But prices steadily improved for passengers. Increasing competition was one important reason, thanks to the US government's opening up of routes in America to smaller competitor airlines, and the rise of charter operators in Europe was another. Some of the old established airlines suffered mortal damage, and in the 1980s and 1990s names such as Braniff and Pan Am disappeared.

British airways Concorde

Your 23-mile-a-minute fact sheet

British airways Concorde

If you are reading this during Concorde's supersonic cruise flight, look at your watch. Check off one minute. During this 60 seconds you have travelled some 23 miles – at twice the height of Mount Everest. Your journey feels little different from subsonic flight at less than half the speed. Yet as a Concorde passenger you are taking part in a new era of aviation history. You may have some questions about this new aircraft and concept of travel. If so here are the answers.

Q How fast are we flying?
A When the machmeter in the cabin is indicating Mach 2 you are flying at twice the speed of sound at Concorde's cruising height of between 50,000ft (15,240m) and 60,000ft (18,250m). This is around 1,320 mph (2,120 kph).
When the machmeter is indicating 0.5 you are travelling at about 380 mph (610 kph), Mach 1 is about 670 mph (1,080 kph) and Mach 1.5 is about 1,000 mph (1,610 kph).

Q What is the cabin altitude in Concorde when it is at cruising height?
A It is equivalent to about 5,550ft (1,700m) compared with 7,550ft (2,290m) of most subsonic passenger jet aircraft. In Concorde you fly higher but it feels lower! The air exchange system is twice as efficient as in most subsonic jets.

In the 1980s and 1990s passenger aeroplanes continued to be refined and improved by manufacturers, but there were no great "quantum leaps". New systems such as fly-by-wire control were introduced in some airliners – the Airbus A-320, for example – but the basic shapes and speeds of transport fleets remained fairly constant. By the 1990s and early 2000s, there were more passengers flying than ever before, but the experience of flying had become for most people akin to train or bus services: useful to their lives in terms of business or holiday travel, but certainly not offering the pulse-quickening glamour of five decades ago.

BELOW The British Airways Concorde fact sheet provided by the airline to passengers on the legendary supersonic airliner. Concorde was the only successful supersonic passenger aircraft. It was operated by both British Airways and Air France.

PREVIOUS PAGE The Boeing 747, being displayed to the public for the first time took place at Everett, Washington on September 30.1968

Charles De Gaulle Airport

A modern airport is a giant transport interchange with hundreds of thousands of people arriving by car, train or bus and departing by aircraft (or vice versa). The largest of these have the same services as a small town, employing thousands of people handling baggage, maintaining security, selling goods, checking passports and carrying out the millions of other duties needed to keep the world on the move. Opened in 1974, Charles de Gaulle in Paris is an archetypal giant international airport and its futuristic design was created specifically for the "jet age". Now, in Europe, only London Heathrow handles more passengers per year.

Q Why are the windows smaller than on other aircraft ?
A They could be larger – and were on prototype aircraft. The present size is to meet varying international technical requirements.

Q Why does the sky appear darker at Concorde's cruising heights ?
A The higher we fly, the less dense the earth's atmosphere. So its effect of scattering the blue elements in the sun's light (very marked at ground level) becomes less. Astronauts observe a black sky in space. And, of course, at Concorde's cruising height the curvature of the earth becomes very apparent.

Q Do passengers notice anything when Concorde goes supersonic ?
A You are the judge of this. It is possible to feel a nudge in the back as the extra thrust through reheat comes in, but the actual passing of Mach 1 is unnoticeable except on the machmeter.

Q What is reheat ?
A The Olympus engines are fitted with afterburners (long used on supersonic aircraft). They burn fuel in the exhaust area of the engines and provide a modest amount of reheat, or power, for take-off and for transonic acceleration.

Q Why is there a droop nose ?
A All delta-wing aircraft have a relatively high angle of incidence (nose-up position) during approach and landing. In Concorde the pitch angle on approach is about 10 degrees up – compared with the 3 degrees of a 747.
Because of this nose-up position improvement of pilot visibility is achieved by moving the nose downward and by lowering the visor. For landing, the nose is in a fully drooped position ($-17\frac{1}{2}$ degrees) which gives the captain on landing better vision than in any subsonic aircraft. For taxiing and take-off it is generally in the intermediate (-5 degrees) drooped position.
A transparent visor is raised during high-speed flight. It gives a clean aerodynamic shape by covering and fairing off the windshields.

Q What is the aircraft's external temperature ?
A Concorde's supersonic cruising speed causes the exterior of the aircraft to heat up through kinetic energy. The temperature at the nose is about 127 degrees Centigrade, at the fuselage and the wings about 92-95 degrees.

Q What is the effect of these high temperatures ?
A Extensive testing has shown that there is no adverse effect whatsoever on the aircraft structure.

Q What is Concorde's landing speed ?
A Not much different from subsonic aircraft – about 160 knots (280 kph).

Q Does there appear to be slight flexing of the fuselage at take-off and in turbulence ?
A All aircraft are built as flexible structures for ultimate strength. There may appear a slight flexing of Concorde's cabin during take-off and in turbulence. This is quite normal, and is similar to the flexing of wings in subsonic aircraft. After more than 5,000 hours of test and endurance flying, Concorde is the most thoroughly proven airliner ever to go into service.

Designed and built by the British Aircraft Corporation and Aerospatiale France, it is powered by four Rolls-Royce (Snecma) Olympus 593 engines designed for Mach 2 cruise. Its length is 203ft 9ins and its span 83ft 10ins.

Q And the Concorde flight crew ?
A Up on the flight deck there is a very experienced captain, co-pilot and flight engineer. The captain and crew present their compliments and wish you a happy journey.

MODERN
AIR POWER

Technological advances made air power even more effective in the late twentieth and early twenty-first centuries. But the huge cost of this technology has meant that the gulf between the air forces of the richest nations and those of the poor has grown enormously. With many of the conflicts in the last 30 years taking place between countries of vastly differing levels of military technology — so-called asymmetrical warfare — it is no surprise that often the results can be overwhelmingly one-sided.

The archetypal modern combat aircraft is expensive, packed with computer equipment and armed with weapons that are themselves more costly than ever before. Arguably the first of this generation of supermachines were the US Navy's F-14 Tomcat and USAF F-15 Eagle, introduced in the mid-1970s. They were more powerful and vastly more advanced in terms of their computer and flight-control systems than anything that had gone before.

A consequence of increasing aircraft cost was the move towards multi-role combat aircraft. Building dedicated fighters, bombers and reconnaissance aircraft was not an option for many governments, hence the development of aircraft such as the Panavia Tornado in the 1970s. Not only was the Tornado designed to carry out the major strike and air defence roles, but its construction was only made possible thanks to international co-operation.

The 1982 Falklands War did not involve the very latest hi-tech combat aircraft, but it did feature the Vertical/Short Take-Off and Landing (V/STOL) Harrier, an ingenious 1960s design that comprehensively defeated Argentina's air force, providing valuable air cover for the British task force sent to reclaim the islands.

The 1991 Gulf War showed just how effective the most advanced aircraft and weapons can be. Some argued that the US-led coalition's demolition of the Iraqi army's ability

RIGHT A Northrop Grumman KC-30 tanker refuels a B-2 Spirit in mid-air during a test flight. Stealth aircraft are very difficult to detect owing to their unusual, angular shape and to the material that covers them. Just as important to modern air forces are the air-to-air refuelling tankers that can keep combat aircraft in the air for many hours, dramatically increasing their range.

OVERLEAF A McDonnell Douglas F-15E Strike Eagle. The F-15E is a multi-role aircraft able to undertake both air-to-ground and air-to-air combat missions. It can carry a variety of different weapons, and variants of the F-15 have been in service with the USAF since the mid-1970s.

Apache AH-64

The Apache is generally regarded as the ultimate ground-support weapon. The first AH-64 entered US Army service in 1984, and around 1,500 have been delivered to date. Nine nations operate, or have selected, the latest variant, the AH-64D, including the UK, Japan and the Netherlands. It is equipped with Hellfire missiles and a 30-millimetre (1.2-inch) automatic cannon, and the crew is assisted in locating targets by laser and infrared systems. The Apache can cruise at up to 284 kilometres per hour (176 miles per hour). Often responding to calls for assistance from troops on the ground, this helicopter has proved extremely effective in modern conflicts such as Afghanistan and Iraq.

to wage war demonstrated that air power could win a war alone – although it was still necessary to send in ground troops to liberate Kuwait. But it was not just the precision "smart bomb" strikes on command and control centres by stealth aircraft such as the F-117, or the destruction of enemy tanks by A-10 Warthogs, nor the direction provided by Airborne Warning and Control (AWACS) aircraft that contributed to victory. Once again, the humble transport aircraft came into its own. C-130s moved coalition forces into and around Saudi Arabia, and in one notable operation, supported the movement of some 250,000 troops into new positions prior to a major attack.

The remarkably low number of coalition casualties in the Gulf War (especially when compared to the Iraqi casualty list) added immeasurably to the perception that air power was a distinctly low-risk method of projecting strength. For example, it was perceived to be more politically expedient (particularly in the United States) to use air strikes to oust Serbia from Kosovo in 1999. Putting troops on the ground would have been extremely unpopular back home. The campaign succeeded in its principle objective with no US or NATO casualties. Today, Unmanned Aerial Vehicles used for a variety of reconnaissance and strike roles reduce the risk of military casualties even further.

The 11 September 2001 terrorist attacks on New York and Washington and the subsequent "War on Terror" led to highly advanced aircraft being used in another "asymmetrical" conflict. Although initial phases of the war against the Taliban in Afghanistan again showed the value of aircraft in modern war, the continued presence of American, British and other coalition troops in that country has demonstrated that a determined and fanatical guerilla force can still prevent technological superpowers from achieving ultimate victory. The lessons were similar in Iraq in 2003. Despite the spectacular "shock and awe" attacks that began the campaign and quick victory in the conventional regime change phase of the war, only a "surge" of troops on the ground eventually began to turn the tide against the insurgents.

ABOVE The Chinese embassy in Belgrade, Yugoslavia (now in Serbia) a year after it was bombed in error by US aircraft in May 1999. NATO blamed the attack on inaccurate targeting information, proving that despite the development of accurate "smart bombs", mistakes that result in the death of innocent civilians can occur, either through systems malfunction or, as in this case, human error.

LEFT U.S. Air Force C 130 cargo plane, Lockheed C-130 Hercules. Capable of using unprepared runways for takeoffs and landings, the C 130 was originally designed as a troop, medical evacuation, and cargo transport aircraft.

Lockheed C-130 Hercules

The C-130 Hercules is the ultimate transport workhorse. Since entering service with the USAF in 1956, variants have served with the air forces of 50 nations. It is an extremely robust aircraft, and can take off from short and unprepared runways. But the most important reason for its longevity is the enormous flexibility of the design. Its main duties are troop and military cargo transport, but in its career the Hercules has also been used as a gunship, a refuelling tanker, a search and rescue platform, and as a humanitarian aid aircraft. It is a key component of any modern army and is set to remain in service for many years to come.

AVIATION
FOR ALL?

The very first aircraft were built neither for war nor for commercial transport. Aviation pioneers were driven to fly by pure curiosity. They persevered because of the novelty and thrill of taking to the air in a machine. Although warfare and transport prompted the biggest advances in aircraft technology, the private flyer — the person who flies for fun, or for personal transport, or to break records — has continued to play a key role in the continuing story of aviation.

Membership of flying clubs grew in the 1920s and 1930s, notably in the United Kingdom. Privately owned aircraft, particularly the de Havilland Moth series, proved extremely popular. Companies such as Beech and Cessna began to create light aircraft specifically for the private individual in the decade immediately preceding the Second World War. In the 1950s, the market for light aircraft grew again and it was in 1955 that the most successful light aircraft ever produced, the Cessna 172, first flew. The third major manufacturer of this type of machine, Piper, also proved that there was a huge desire for light aircraft – either used as personal transport or as real leisure craft. Bridging the gap between the small light aircraft and a large commercial airliner is the personal business jet. This most luxurious of executive accessories has, since the 1960s, come to symbolize individual wealth or corporate power.

However, the dream of true "aviation for all" has remained out of reach. At the most fanciful end of the spectrum, the idea of a

BELOW A Cessna 180. Cessna is one of the most familiar names in general aviation. Since the late 1920s, the company has produced a series of leisure and light transport aircraft including the Cessna 172, one of the most popular light aircraft ever built.

Bombardier Learjet

The classic epitome of executive transport is, unarguably, the Learjet. Developed by William Lear in the 1960s from a fighter-bomber design, the Learjet excelled in terms of performance. It was faster than earlier private aircraft and could operate at higher altitude than many airliners. The first variant, the Learjet 23, flew from Los Angeles to New York and back in just over 11-and-a-half hours and later models set many other impressive speed and performance records. Although other manufacturers – such as Dassault in the 1970s and Gulfstream in the 1990s – created very successful executive models, the Learjet has maintained its position thanks to its continually developed and improved design.

BELOW Dick Rutan and Jeana Yeager with their record-breaking round-the-world-aircraft *Voyager* in December 1985. Dick Rutan's brother, Burt, designed *Voyager* and went on to be responsible for several other truly remarkable machines, including *SpaceShip One*, the first privately developed spacecraft to successfully reach space.

flying car has continued to appeal, but one has yet to materialize as a viable vehicle. Kit aeroplanes were seen as a more realistic way to open up powered flight to the masses. Possibly the first of such machines were Henri Mignet's 1930s "Flying Fleas". Although initially popular, they were banned as unsafe by both the British and French governments. "Kit planes" similar to the Fleas have flown since and continue to fly today, but they are subject to very stringent regulations.

Light aircraft have to follow many of the same rules as military or commercial aircraft and this has served to remove much of the spontaneity from flight. Perhaps the closest to a reasonably cheap and available mode of leisure flight is the glider. Gliding offers a much less expensive way to experience the thrill of flight; and one that is less restricted by the rules that regulate light aircraft. The popularity of hot air balloons, hang-gliders, gliders, microlights, powered parachutes and sky diving demonstrates that even in the age of mass travel, the appeal of flight simply for its own sake is still very strong.

The extremely high cost of modern hi-tech aircraft makes it beyond the means of most private citizens to set some of the historically more prestigious records. "Blue riband" feats are invariably left to those with government backing. For example, the current absolute world speed record belongs to the USAF crew of a Lockheed SR-71 Blackbird. But the pioneer spirit of the early aeronauts lives on in today's record-breaking aviators.

They have found other ways to push the boundaries, particularly setting distance and endurance records. Notable modern adventurers include Dick Rutan and Jeana Yeager, who flew round the world non-stop in 1986, and record-setting balloonist Per Lindstrand. These modern feats often capture the public imagination – perhaps because it is the person, rather than the machine, that is placed at the centre of the achievement.

OPPOSITE Hot air balloons soar at the Albuquerque International Balloon Fiesta, New Mexico, USA in 2008. Balloon festivals are popular all over the world, with ever more outlandish designs being constructed.

OVERLEAF Hang-gliding over Yosemite Valley. Hang-gliding is possibly the closest we can get today to experiencing the true freedom of flight.

Steve Fossett
(1944–2007)

Born in Tennessee, Fossett made his fortune in stockbroking. He ploughed much of his wealth into the pursuit of records and set over 100, some on land, some at sea and many in the air. In 2005, he made the first solo non-stop round-the-world flight, and in 2006 he set the record for the longest flight (almost 77 hours, covering over 40,000 kilometres [25,000 miles]). Most famously, in 2002, he became the first man to complete a solo circumnavigation of the globe in a balloon. Fossett's achievements were recognized in 2007 when he was inducted into the American National Aviation Hall of Fame.

AVIATION
AND THE MODERN WORLD

At the beginning of the twentieth century, many bold claims were made about the effect aviation might have on our lives. Some said it would make warfare obsolete; surely no nation would be so foolish as to go to war when its own cities and people would be so vulnerable to retaliatory attack? Others predicted that it would bring the peoples of the world together. More pessimistic prognosticators, perhaps influenced by the H G Wells classic novel *The War in the Air*, believed that aircraft as ultimate weapons could spell the end of civilization. In truth, aviation has been a mixed blessing, helping some and bringing harm to others.

At the start of the twenty-first century, it is important to remember just how large an industry aviation is. It employs hundreds of thousands of people worldwide, building, servicing, flying, and supporting aircraft. The craft themselves are so expensive to produce that, more often than not, international co-operation is the only viable way to build them. Even the United States makes use of international contractors to supply systems for state-of-the-art aircraft. One consolation of this massive expenditure is the increased length of operational service. Aircraft built in the first half of the twentieth century were often obsolete within a few years, whilst an air force or airline today can now expect to obtain decades of work from a modern technological marvel.

In parts of the developing world where problems are often substantially more challenging than those faced in the West, aircraft can have a dramatically positive impact. In areas made unreachable by conventional land-transport following crises such as war or natural disaster, aircraft can be used to deliver vital food and medical supplies.

Aviation makes vast inhospitable places habitable; aircraft of the Australian Royal Flying Doctor Service for example, can mean the difference between life and death in remote areas. And it is not just in the Australian bush that aircraft can play such a vital role. Modern

BELOW Loading cargo at night, Cologne-Bonn airport Germany, 2007. Every year freight companies deliver hundreds of millions of packages to customers all around the world via both dedicated cargo aircraft and in the holds of passenger aeroplanes. Just two of the largest freight companies between them deliver around 18 million packages every day.

OVERLEAF An air/sea rescue helicopter assists a vessel in distress in 2006. In 2007 in the UK, RAF and Royal Navy rescue helicopters were called out over 1,750 times, assisting around 1,500 people.

Airbus A-380

The Airbus A-380 is the largest commercial airliner in service today; the ultimate "economy of scale" transport, it is equipped to carry over 500 passengers. European consortium Airbus Industries produced a series of successful airliners in the 1980s and 1990s, and the A-380 was designed as a "hub and spoke" aircraft to fly between major airports. Owing to its enormous size, the A-380 can only operate at very large airports which have been upgraded to cope with its bulk and wingspan. American company Boeing has invested in a smaller design, the Boeing 787, which although only able to carry around half of the passengers of an A-380, may consequently prove to be a more flexible option as it offers the potential to operate from a greater number of airports.

ABOVE Airport expansion is a controversial and divisive issue. While many argue that increased capacity is necessary to satisfy the rising public demand for air travel, protests often centre on environmental concerns about the impact of more flights on climate change, and the fears of local people who are concerned about increased noise and air pollution.

ABOVE Pakistani policemen unload supplies from a US transport helicopter in Kashmir in 2005 after a devastating earthquake. In the wake of this huge natural disaster, helicopters provided one of the best means of supplying aid to villages in the affected areas. They were also used to evacuate injured people.

air ambulances are able to transport critically injured patients to hospital within minutes, and the lives of numerous climbers and mariners have been saved by rescue helicopters and air-sea rescue crews.

For many of us, our involvement with flying is limited to holiday or business travel. We can also keep in regular and close contact with family and friends spread across the world, thanks to the network of air routes that criss-cross the planet. We are increasingly accustomed to the ready availability of imported products, the delivery of which is often time-dependent. The range of items that are transported by air is staggering – from fresh flowers to computer equipment, from exotic fruit to the mail.

However, it is inevitable that when so many people can fly to so many destinations, problems may result. Some locations around the world gain enormous benefit from visiting travellers, but others face unwelcome and sometimes crippling over-development thanks to unrestricted and unsustainable tourism. Perhaps most alarmingly of all, aviation is one of the fastest growing producers of the gases that cause the greenhouse effect. An overwhelming body of evidence shows

that this is having a devastating impact on our planet. One of the most enduring and horrifying images of recent times was the sight of passenger aeroplanes flying into the World Trade Center in New York, and the Pentagon in Washington. Although the use of aircraft by terrorists is mercifully a rare occurrence – thanks in part to the increased levels of security at most modern airports – there is another equally sobering aspect of their existence: they make national and even natural borders unimportant. While this is a tremendous boon for travellers, it can be a terrifying prospect for the civilians who, since the First World War, have been placed in the front line of battle, thanks to the awesome power of aerial bombardment.

ABOVE AND RIGHT The 11 September 2001 attacks on the World Trade Center in New York, USA. Nearly 3,000 people died when terrorists crashed four hijacked airliners into the World Trade Center, the Pentagon in Washington and a field in Pennsylvania.

Eurofighter Typhoon

The Eurofighter Typhoon in many ways symbolizes the modern aircraft industry. Although it was originally designed during the Cold War, because of an extremely lengthy development process, it did not enter service until over a decade after the fall of the Berlin Wall in 1989 and the end of communism in the Soviet Union. The product of four countries working in collaboration (Britain, Germany, Italy and Spain), Eurofighter parts are built all over Europe, with final assembly taking place in every one of the partner nations. The design has by necessity changed and evolved, so that what was once intended as a pure fighter now fulfils many other combat roles, including bombing and reconnaissance.

INDEX

Page numbers in italic type refer to pictures or their captions.

A

Achilles, HMS 96

Ader, Clément 10, 12
Aerodrome 18
Aérospatiale Concorde 136, 136, 137
Afghanistan 138, 143
air ambulances 155
airborne warfare 93
Airborne WARning and Control (AWACS) 143
Airbus
  A-320 137
  A380 150, 151
aircraft carriers 46, 46, 96, 96, 101
Aircraft Manufacturing Company (Airco) 35
air defence systems 42
airliners 35, 72–5, 73, 74–5, 108–13, 109, 110, 111, 112–13
  jet 132–7, 132, 133, 134–5, 136, 137
airlines
  Air France 61
  American Airlines 72, 74–5
  Braniff 136
  British Airways 136, 136, 137
  British Overseas Airways Corporation (BOAC) 61, 108, 111, 112–13
  Eastern Airlines 72
  government subsidies 61, 108
  Imperial Airways 57, 60–1, 71, 71, 73, 74
  KLM 110
  Lufthansa 61, 76
  Pan Am 70–1, 71, 108, 132, 136
  Robertson Aircraft Corporation 72
  Trans World Airlines (TWA) 72, 72, 111, 111, 113
  United Air Lines 72
air mail 57, 58, 61, 72
airmobile tactics 123
air/sea rescue 152–3
airships 8, 10, 31, 42, 42, 46, 52–3, 67, 68
Albatros 31
  DIII 41
Alcock, John 50, 53, 53, 55
Aldrin, Buzz 129, 131
America flying boat 50
Anderson, Rudolf 117, 117
Antoinette IV 23
Apollo missions 127, 129, 130, 131
Argus, HMS 46
Ark Royal, HMS 96
Arlandes, Marquis d' 8, 9

Armstrong, Neil 129, 131
Armstrong Whitworth
  Argosy 57
  AW27 Ensign 73, 74
asymmetrical warfare 138, 143
Atlantis space shuttle 131
autogyros 105
Aviatik 31
Avion III 11
Avro 27, 31
  Lancaster 86, 87, 87
  Lancastrian 108
  Vulcan 114
  York 114

B

Baldwin, Stanley 84
Ball, Albert 39
ballistic missiles 116–17, 117, 129
balloons
  hot air 8, 9, 10, 146, 147
  hydrogen 8
  observation 33, 35
barnstormers 59
barrage balloons 42
Battle of the Atlantic 101
Battle of Britain 46, 79, 80–5, 80, 81, 82–3, 84, 85
Beech 145
Bell Aircraft
  UH-1 Huey 120
  X-1 105
Bell, Alexander Graham 26
Berlin Airlift 114, 115
biplanes 20
Bismarck 96
Blanchard, Jean-Pierre 8
Bleriot, Louis 20–5, 21, 22–3, 24, 25, 26, 29, 31, 65
Bleriot VII 21
Bleriot XI 21, 22–3, 22–3
blimps 46
Blitz 80–5, 80, 81, 82–3, 84, 85
Blitzkrieg 78, 79
"Bloody April" 41
Boddington, Christopher Bindloss 85
Boeing 72
  247 72, 74
  307 Stratoliner 75
  314 Clipper 70, 70–1, 71
  377 Stratocruiser 109, 113, 113
  707 132, 132
  727 136
  737 136
  747 Jumbo Jet 134, 134–5, 136
  787 150
  2707 136
  AH-64 Apache 138, 138
  B-17 Flying Fortress 87, 87
  B-29 Superfortress 88, 114, 120
  B-47 45, 114

B-52 Stratofortress 114, 123, 123
bomber aircraft 117
  Korea and Vietnam 120, 123
  multi-role aircraft 138
  World War I 35, 42–5, 42, 43, 44, 46, 49
  World War II 78, 79, 80–5, 82–3, 86–9, 86–7, 88–9
Bomber Command 86, 88, 93
Bouchier, Hélène 59, 59
Braun, Wernher von 126, 129, 129
Breguet 31
Breguet, Louis 105
Bristol Aeroplane Company 31
  Blenheim 79
  Britannia 111
British Aircraft Corporation
  Concorde 136, 136, 137
  One-Eleven 136
Brown, Arthur Whitten 50, 53, 53, 54–5, 55
Byrd, Richard 64

C

Camm, Sydney 81
Campaign for Nuclear Disarmament (CND) 118–19
cantilevered wings 49
Caproni bomber 44
Carpenter, M Scott 126
carpet-bombing 123
Caudron CL 450 59
Cayley, Sir George 10, 12, 12, 13
Cernan, Gene 129
Cessna 145
  172 145, 145
  180 144–5
Chain Home radar 84
Challenger space shuttle 131, 131
Chamberlain, Clarence 64
Chanute, Octave 12
Charles de Gaulle Airport 137, 137
Charles, Jacques 8
Chicago Convention 108
Chindits 93
Churchill, Winston 70, 81, 84
circumnavigation, World 58
Clostermann, Pierre Henri 93, 93
Cobham, Alan 57, 57, 58
Cold War 105, 114–19, 120, 123, 126
Colli, François 62
Collins, Michael 131
Cologne 88
Columbia space shuttle 131, 131
Concorde 136, 136, 137
Coningham, Sir Arthur 93, 93
Consolidated
  B-24 bomber 106–7
  PB4Y-1 Liberator 98–9
  PBY Catalina 96
Convair

B-36 Peacemaker 114
  F-106 117
Cooper, Gordon 126
Coral Sea, Battle of the 101
La Croix de Sud 58
Cuban Missile Crisis 117
Curtiss
  JN-4 26, 59
  Model D 26
  NC-4 50, 50–1
  SB2C Helldiver 101
Curtiss, Glen 26, 26, 28, 50

D

Dam Busters 86
Dassault 146
  Mirage 107
  Mystère 107
  Ouragan 105
Dassault, Marcel 107, 107
Dayton-Wright Airplane Company 48–9
D-Day 93
de Havilland 35
  Aeroplane Hire Service 57
  Comet 35, 132, 133
  DH 2 36
  DH 9A 56
  DH 16 56, 56
  DH 50 50
  DH 66 Hercules 57
  DH 91 Albatross 74
  Mosquito 35, 87, 90
  Moth 35, 145
  Puss Moth 64
de Havilland, Geoffrey 32, 35, 35
  BE2 32, 32, 41
  BE2c 32
Discovery space shuttle 131
dog-fights 49, 84, 121
Doolittle Raid 101
Dornier Wals 69
Douglas Aircraft Company
  A-1 Skyraider 120
  C-47 Skytrain 75, 92, 114
  C-54 Skymaster 115
  C-74 Globemaster 114
  DC-1 72
  DC-2 72
  DC-3 74–5, 74–5, 111, 113
  DC-6 111, 113
  DC-7 110, 111
  DC-8 132
  DC-9 136
  SBD Dauntless 101
  Skysleeper 75
  World Cruiser 58
Douglas, Donald 111, 111
Douhet, Giulio 44
Dowding, Sir Hugh 84, 84
Dresden 86, 86, 88
Dunning, E H 46, 46

E

Earhart, Amelia 64, 65
Eckener, Hugo 68, 68
electronic warfare 123
Elliot, Arthur 58
Endeavour space shuttle 131
English Channel 20–5, 20, 22
English Electric Lightning 117
Éole 10, 12
Esnault-Pelterie, Robert 20
Eurofighter Typhoon 154, 155
Explorer I satellite 129

F

Fabre, Henri 28
factory production 29, 31, 32, 46–9, 47, 48–9
  World War II 102, 104, 106–7
Fairchild Republic A-10 Thunderbolt "Warthog" 143
Fairey Aviation Company
  Battle 79
  Seafox 96
  Swordfish 96
Falklands War 138
Farman 31
  Goliath 44
Farman, Henri 20, 26, 29
Fieseler Storch 90
fighter aircraft
  interceptors 117
  interrupter mechanism 36
  jet engines 120, 121
  Korean War 120, 123
  multi-role aircraft 138
  piston engines 123
  pusher designs 36
  Vietnam War 123
  World War I 36–41, 36–7, 38–9, 41, 46, 49
  World War II 76, 79, 81, 85
flight attendants 75, 111, 133
float planes 58
fly-by-wire 137
flying boats 26, 28, 46, 50, 56, 58, 70–1, 70–1, 96, 102
Flying Circus 39, 41
Flying Doctor Service 150
"Flying Flea" 146
Focke, Heinrich 105
Fokker 31, 72
  DrI triplane 39
  D VII 41
  Eindecker 36
  FVIIB-3m 64
Fokker, Anthony 47
Ford
  Trimotor 58, 72
  Willow Run plant 106–7
Fossett, Steve 146, 146
France
  Aéronautique Militaire 31, 36, 41, 41
Free French Air Force 93
Friendship 64

Furious, HMS 46, 46

G

Gagarin, Yuri 129
Garrison, Vermont 123, 123
Garros, Roland 26, 36
Gatty, Harold 58
Germany
  German Army Air Service 31, 39, 39, 41
    Lufftwaffe 76–9, 77, 80–5, 90, 93
Gibson, Guy 86
Giffard, Henri 10
Glenn, John 126
gliders 10, 12, 93, 146
Gloster Meteor 105
Goodyear 68
Gordon, Lew 64
Göring, Herman 47
Gotha bomber 42
  GIV 44
Graf Spee 96
Graham-White, Claude 28
Grand Prix d'Aviation 20
Grissom, Virgil 126
Grossflugzeug 44
Grumman F-14 Tomcat 138
Guernica 76, 77
Gulfstream 146
Gulf War (1991) 138, 143
Guyenmer, George 40, 41, 41

H

Handly Page 31, 50, 55
  0/100 44
  0/400 43, 44
  Hastings 114
  HP42 73, 74
  V/1500 44
  Victor 114
hang-gliders 8, 11, 146, 148–9
Harrier Jump Jet 138
Harris, Sir Arthur 86, 88, 88
Hawker 53
  Hurricane 79, 80, 81, 93, 104
  Tempest 93
  Typhoon 93, 94–5
Hawker, Harry 50, 53, 53
Heart's Content 64
Heinkel HE 111 84
helicopters 102, 105, 120, 122, 123, 154
  air/sea rescue 152–3
  Bell UH-1 Huey 120
  Boeing AH-64 Apache 138, 138
  Sikorsky 102, 102–3, 105
Hendon 28
Heyser, Richard S 117
Hiroshima 88, 88
Hitler, Adolf 76, 77, 84
Hughes Aircraft Company 72
  H-1 72
  H-4 Hercules 72

Hughes, Howard 72, 72
humanitarian aid 143, 154
"Hump" 93
Hydravia 28

I

Illustrious, HMS 96
Ilyushin IL 2 Shturmovik 91, 93
Independent Air Force (IAF) 44, 49
interceptors 117
Intercontinental Ballistic Missiles (ICBMs) 116–17, 129
International Air Transport Association (IATA) 108
International Space Station 128–9
Iraq 143

J

Jagdgeschwader 1 (JG1) 41
Japan 76
  atomic bombs 88, 88
  bombing of Shanghai 78
  kamikaze 101
  Pearl Harbor 97, 97, 100, 101
Jeffries, John 8
jet engine 35, 102, 105, 105, 113, 120, 121
  passenger aircraft 132–7, 132, 133, 134–5, 136, 137
Johnson, Amy 64, 65, 65
Johnson, Clarence "Kelly" 111, 114, 114
June Bug 26
Junkers
  Ju 4 49
  Ju 8 49
  Ju 87 "Stuka" 79, 79
  Ju 88 84

K

kamikaze 101
Kennedy, John F 117, 129
kit aeroplanes 146
kites 8, 8
Korean War 120, 123, 123
Korolev, Sergei 129, 131, 131
Kosovo 143, 143
Krushchev, Nikita 117
Kuwait 143

L

Langly, Samuel Pierpont 12, 18, 18
Latécoère 69
Latham, Hubert 20, 23, 26
Learjet 146, 146
Lear, William 146
Levine, Charles 64
Lexington, USS 101
Leyte Gulf, Battle of 101

Lilienthal, Otto 8, 11, 12, 14
Lindbergh, Charles 62, 62, 63, 64, 64, 66–7, 72
Lindstrand, Per 146
Lockheed 113, 114
  14 Super Electra 72
  C-69 111
  C-130 Hercules 142–3, 143
  Constellation series 111, 111, 113, 114
  F-104 Starfighter 114
  F-117 143
  L-049 111
  L-1049 Super-Constellation 111, 113
  L-1649 Starliner 113
  P-38 Lightening 93, 97, 114
  P-80 jet 114
  SR-71 114, 117, 146
  TriStar 136
  U2 114, 117
  Vega 58
  Vega Gull 64
Loerzer, Bruno 47
loop the loop 26
Los Angeles, USS 68

M

McDonnell Douglas 113
  DC-10 136
  F-4 Phantom 120, 124–5
  F-15 Eagle 138
  F-15E Strike Eagle 140–1
Mackenzie-Grieve, Kenneth 50
Manhattan project 107
Manly, Charles 18
Martin 53, 111
  130 Philippine Clipper 69
Martinsyde 50, 53
Maxim, Hiram 12
Mermoz, Jean 58, 59
Messerschmitt Bf 109 76, 80
Messerschmitt, Willy 80
microlight aircraft 146
Midway, Battle of 101
Mignet, Henri 146
Mikoyan-Gurevich MiG-15 120, 120, 123
Milch, Erhard 76, 76
military transport 120
Minuteman 116–17
Mir space stations 131
Mitchell, Billy 44
Mitchell, R J 56
Mollinson, Jim 64, 65, 65
monoplanes 8
Montgolfier Brothers 8, 9, 10
Morane-Saulnier MS 406 79
Morgan, Fax 53
Mussolini, Benito 76
Mutually Assured Destruction 114

N

Nagasaki 88

napalm 123
National Aeronautics and Space Administration (NASA) 129, 131
naval warfare 96–101
New York to Paris 62–7, 62, 63, 66
Nieuport 31, 41
  Scout 36
Nimitz, Admiral Chester 101, 101
Noonan, Fred 65
North American Aviation
  F-86 Sabre 120, 121
  P-51 Mustang 88–9, 93, 120, 123
North Atlantic Treaty Organisation (NATO) 117
Northcliffe, Lord 50
Northrop Grumman
  B-2 Spirit 139
  KC-30 139
nuclear weapons 88, 88, 102, 107, 114, 117, 118–19, 123
Nungesser, Charles 62

O

Ohain, Otto von 105
Oppenheimer, Robert 107
Orteig, Raymond 62
Overlord, Operation 93

P

Pacific War 97, 97, 100, 101
package tours 136
Panavia Tornado 138
parachutes 32, 92, 93
  powered 146
Parasol Morane 41
passenger services 55, 56, 56, 58, 58, 60–1, 61, 108–13, 108, 109, 110, 111, 112–13
  airliners 35, 72–5, 73, 74–5
  air ships 68, 69
  Boeing 314 Clipper 70, 70–1
  jet airliners 132–7, 132, 133, 134–5, 136, 137
  see also airlines
Pearl Harbor 97, 97, 100, 101
Pégoud, Adolphe 26
Perreyon, Edmond 26
Philippine Sea, Battle of the 101, 101
photo-reconnaissance 35, 90, 93
Pilâtre de Rozier, Jean-François 8, 9
Piper 145
  Cub 90
piston engine 113, 123
Pixton, Harold 31
Polaris 117
Post, Wiley 58
Powers, Gary 117
Prévost, Marcel 26
Project Mercury 126
propellers 18

Q

Quimby, Harriet 28

R

R 34 airship 52–3, 55, 68
R 100 airship 68
R 101 airship 68
radar 80, 84, 102, 105
Raynham, Freddie 50, 53
Read, Albert C 50
reconnaissance aircraft 32, 33, 35, 36, 46, 90, 90, 93, 96, 114, 117
  unmanned 143
refuelling, in-flight 56, 139
Richthofen, Manfred von 35, 39, 39
Rickenbacker, Edward V 38–9
River Plate, Battle of the 96
rockets 102
  space exploration 126–31
Roe, Alliot Verdon 27
Roe II 27
Rolling Thunder, Operation 120
Rolls-Royce Merlin 81
Roosevelt, Franklin D 70, 100
Royal Aircraft Factory 35
  BE2 32, 32, 41
  BE2c 32
  SE5a 41, 46–7
Royal Air Force (RAF) 31, 44, 46–7, 49, 76, 79, 80, 80, 81, 82, 83, 84, 85, 86–8, 90, 93
Royal Flying Corps (RFC) 31, 36, 41, 49, 55
Royal Naval Air Service (RNAS) 31, 42, 46, 46
Roy, Gladys 59
R-plane 42
Rumpler 31
Russian Army Air Service 31
Rutan, Burt 146
Rutan, Dick 146, 146
Ryan Aeronautical 62

S

Saint-Exupéry, Antoine de 59
Salyut programme 131
Santos-Dumont, Alberto 20, 21
satellites 129
Saturn V 127
Saulnier, Raymond 22
Schirra, Wally 126
Schneider Trophy 31, 56
Scott, G H 55
seaplanes 28, 29, 56
September 11 attacks 143, 155
Shanghai, Japanese bombing 78
Shaw, USS 97
Shepard, Alan 126, 129
ships, take-off from 26, 46
Shōkaku 101
Short Brothers 28, 50
  S-23 C-Class 71, 71
  S-25 Sunderland 114

Shütte-Lanzes 42
Sikorsky
    Il'ya Muromets 31, 102
    R-4 Hoverfly 105
    VS-300 102, 102–3, 105
Sikorsky, Igor 31, 102, 105
sky diving 146
Skylab space station 131
Slayton, Donald 126
"smart" weapons 123, 143, 143
Sopwith 30, 31, 50, 53
    Camel 36–7, 41, 53
    Pup 46, 46, 53
    Tabloid 31, 53
space exploration 102, 126–31
SpaceShip One 146
Space Shuttle 131, 131
Spad XIII 41
Spanish Civil War 76, 77
Speer, Albert 88
Spirit of St Louis 62, 62, 63, 64
Sputnik satellite 129
Stalin, Joseph 93
stealth aircraft 139, 143
strafing 35, 46
Strasser, Peter 44, 44
stratosphere 75
Stulz, Wilmer 64
submarines 46
Sud Aviation Caravelle 132, 136
Supermarine
    S6B 56
    Spitfire 80, 81, 84, 90
supersonic aircraft 136, 136, 137
Surface-to-Air Missiles (SAMs)
    117

T

Taranto, Battle of 97
Taylor, Charlie 18
Taylorcraft Auster 90
thousand bomber raids 88
tourism 136, 155
Transatlantic flights 50–5, 50–1,
    52–3, 54–5, 62–7, 66–7
Treaty of Versailles 76
Trenchard, General Hugh 44,
    49, 49
triplanes 27
Trippe, Juan 71
Tupolev
    Tu-95 114
    Tu-144 136
turbojet 105
turboprop 113, 114

U

Unger, Ivan 59
United States Air Mail 61, 72
United States Army Air Force
    (USAAF) 86–7
United States Army Air Service
    (USAAS) 38–9, 72
Unmanned Aerial Vehicles 143

V

V1 flying bomb 84
V2 rocket 84, 126

V-bombers 114
Vertical/Short Take-Off and
    Landing (V/STOL) 138
Vickers 41, 50
    R 100 68
    Valiant 114
    Vimy 44, 53, 53, 55
    Viscount 113
Vietnam War 120, 122, 123,
    124–5
Voisin Brothers 20, 21, 29, 29, 31
Voyager 146

W

Wallis, Barnes 68, 87
War on Terror 143
Watson-Watt, Robert 105
Wells, H G
    The War in the Air 42, 150
Western Desert Air Force 93
Whittle, Sir Frank 105, 105
wind tunnel 18
wing warping 14, 23
Winnie Mae 58
World Trade Center 155, 155
World War I 31, 32–49
World War II 71, 76–107
Wright Brothers 7, 12, 14–19,
    14, 15, 16, 17, 20, 23, 28
Wright Flyer 17, 18, 20
Wright Whirlwind J-5C 62

Y

Yamamoto, Admiral Isoroku 97,
    97
Yeager, Chuck 105
Yeager, Jeana 146, 146
Yorktown, USS 96, 101

Z

Zeppelin 31, 42, 42, 44, 55, 68
    Graf Zeppelin 68, 69
    Hindenburg 68, 69
Zeppelin, Count Ferdinand von
    28, 31
Zero fighter 97
Zuikaku 101

TRANSLATIONS

Page 61: Imperial Airways Brochure
What Imperial Airways can do for Messageries Maritimes passengers.
How flying with Imperial Airways can help Messageries Maritimes passengers.
You may be an experienced traveller, but perhaps you still haven't realised how using Imperial Airways can help you gain some time.

GO TO MADAGASCAR BY PLANE: The quickest way to go from Europe to Madagascar or Mauritius is undoubtedly by taking an Imperial Airways plane to Nairobi, going from Nairobi to Mombasa by train, and then catching the Messageries Maritimes liner. For the fastest route from the Cape, it's Imperial Airways and Messageries Maritimes again, via Nairobi and Mombasa.

TAKE A PLANE TO THE CAPE: You can travel from any Mediterranean port on a Messageries Maritimes liner, get off at Alexandria, and you can be in Khartoum in a day, in Nairobi in three days and at the Cape in seven days.

TAKE A PLANE TO THE FAR EAST: Imperial Airways also operates routes to the Indies. These link up with the Messageries Maritimes passenger liners, and they can also shorten your journey to the Far East by several days.

MAP: The map opposite shows you where these services fly to and the nearest points on the routes to the ports where the Messageries Maritimes ships call.

AIR TRAVEL IS COMFORTABLE: Don't imagine that air passengers have to rough it. Not at all! They travel in luxury. Imperial Airways operate the largest planes in service on regular airline routes, and the passenger accommodation is as quiet and comfortable as a Pullman carriage. All our planes have washrooms and spacious baggage holds. This is the way to travel – no dust, no stifling heat. Just sit back and enjoy the cool, fast flight. It won't tire you out – there's no stress and strain. That's why air travel is perfect for women and children, and for the elderly and the infirm.

(Caption to photo) An "Atalanta" - one of the planes waiting to take you to Africa and the Far East.

(Text above map) HOW IMPERIAL AIRWAYS SERVICES CONNECT UP WITH MESSAGERIES MARITIMES' ROUTES

(Text in map:
"Routes des Messageries Maritimes" = "Messageries Maritimes routes",
"Routes de l'Imperial Airways" = « Imperial Airways routes »)
(Text below map, which runs over into the next page)
Ask at the purser's office for our illustrated brochures and timetables.

A COMFORTABLE BED ON TERRA FIRMA EVERY NIGHT: When you travel on Imperial Airways' Empire routes, you can sleep in a comfortable bed every night. The hotel accomodation and the meals (and even the tips!) are included in the Imperial Airways fares – and they're really low. You can fly across Africa or go to the Indies with jut a few francs in your pocket for unforeseen expenses. As they say – no hidden extras!

AIR FARES: Here are just a few examples of Imperial Airways' prices. But prices may change, so to find out the latest situation, just check in the brochures published by Imperial Airways – available in all branches of Messageries Maritimes or Imperial Airways, or from any good travel agents.

Alexandria to…	Single fare	Return fare
Paris	£38	£68 8
Baghdad	£27	£48 12
Karachi	£60	£108 0
Calcutta	£85	£157 0
Rangoon	£98	£176 8
Khartoum	£31	£55 16
Nairobi	£75	£135 00
The Cape	£102	£183 12

N. B. All payments must be made in Sterling (pounds, shillings and pence)

AIR TRAVEL IS SAFE: Travelling on Imperial Airways' big planes is so safe that the accident insurance premiums are the same as they would be if you were travelling by road. And if you're sending goods by air freight, the insurance rates are actually lower than they are for road haulage. But that only applies to Imperial Airways – not with any other airline!

DAILY SERVICES: In addition to its Empire routes, Imperial Airways can also offer you a comfortable flight to Europe. During the Summer months, there are five flights a day in each direction between Paris and London (three a day in Winter). All the planes operating on this route are "Heracles", the largest aircraft flying on regular services anywhere in the world. They can carry 38 passengers, and they have buffets and washrooms. Our flight attendants will serve you hot or cold meals. In Summer, you can fly from London to Paris and then catch a connecting flight to Basle or Zurich. There's a daily two-way service all the year round linking London, Brussels and Cologne. And Imperial Airways flights connect with services provided by other airlines. So you can start your journey by sea with Messageries Maritimes, then transfer to an aircraft and go anywhere in Europe.

MAKING RESERVATIONS: To obtain timetables, or for any other information, contact the ship's purser, or apply to Imperial Airways, Airways House, 38, Avenue de l'Opéra, Paris. Telephone: Opéra 09-16 (day and night). Telegrams: Flying, Paris

(Caption to photo) A "Heracles" – one of the planes waiting to fly you from Paris to London

Page 66–7T: Aéro Club de France report on Lindbergh's record-breaking New York to Paris flight. NB. Text in italics indicates handwriting.

AÉRO-CLUB DE FRANCE, AVIATION COMMISSION, 35, rue François-1er, 35 – PARIS

OFFICIAL REPORT(1): *New York – Paris. Straight line distance record. Raymond Orteig Prize.*

BACKGROUND INFORMATION
Name of senior official commissioner. *Chief engineer Hirschauer Secretary of Competitions Commission of Aéro Club de France*
Names of other official commissioners:
Names of deputy commissioners:
Member of (2)
Name of timekeeper(s):
Description of site of event (3): *Le Bourget airfield, Paris*
(1) Indicate nature of sporting event or record attempt. The official report should be sent to the Aéro-Club de France within 24 hours of the completion of the event.
(2) Indicate society to which commissioners belong. Indicate whether supervision was the responsibility of the Aéro-Club de France or of a society appointed for this purpose.
(3) Give brief description of course; attach a simple sketch with dimensions. This could usefully be on page 4 of this official report, showing the main dimensions, the positioning of the marker posts, their respective distances, etc.. Indicate the direction of travel (which way the competitors were going).
Indicate PRECISELY how the Commissioner measured the course.
DETAILS OF EVENT(4)
Location of approved commissioners, deputy commissioners or monitors(5):
On site, opposite airport administration building
Name of competitor: *Charles Lindbergh*
Nationality: *American*
Date and place of birth:
Air pilot's licence no.:
Licence year no.:
Characteristics of aircraft(6): *Ryan monoplane, Wright 240 hp engine*
Test apparatus used (if applicable)(7): *Sealed recording barograph no. 353.*
Six-hour cylinder, manufactured by Hue(?), Paris
(4) When there are several competitors, a special official report should be drawn up for each of them.
(5) Also indicate on sketch the position of the supervisors within the location. As a general rule, there should be a commissioner at each post.
(6) Number of plane surfaces, size, length, engine (manufacturer's name and power), number and position of propellers. This information (useful on any documentation) will also make it possible to verify that the machine is actually in the class laid down for the event.
(7) Indicate whether this apparatus was provided by the competitor and approved by the commission, or laid down by them. Indicate what condition it was in initially, and

confirm that it was sealed.
BRIEF REPORT OF EVENT
Departure time(8): *Roosevelt Field – Long Island. 6.51 a.m. and 30 seconds*
(U. S. time), New York. 20th May, 1927
Arrival time(8): *Le Bourget – Paris. 10.22 p.m.* (official French time). 21st May, 1927
Distance travelled(9): *5850 kilometres. Approximately five thousand, eight hundred and fifty kilometres (the exact distance is to be measured by the National Aeronautic Association).*
Miscellaneous(10): *The barograph's seal had not been clamped. The machine had six tanks, namely five petrol tanks (three in plane surfaces and two in the fuselage), and an oil tank. The three petrol tanks in the plane surfaces had been sealed. The seals had been clamped, but without any marks. The two petrol tanks in the fuselage and the oil tank had not been sealed* (observations made in presence of (?)). *The competitor had no parachute. Upon arrival, the tanks were found to contain: 322 litres of petrol. 57 litres of oil.*
(8) The time indicated shall be the official time in the country where the event takes place: Paris time, Western European Time, etc..
(9) Indicate names of first and last marker posts passed in full flight.
(10) In particular, indicate whether the competitor missed one or more marker posts and, in that case, whether he made a complete circuit of these posts. In a general manner, indicate all irregularities (or incidents which might give rise to objections), any objections, etc.. Give names of witnesses, if applicable. In particular, indicate whether the inspection apparatus has functioned satisfactorily.
20th/21st May, 1927. New York – Paris. World distance record. Raymond Orteig Prize. (Signatures) The competitor: *Charles Lindbergh.* Senior approved commissioner: *Chief engineer (L. Hirschauer)*
The official report should be dated and signed by the senior commissioner, the approved commissioners and deputy commissioners and the time-keeper(s).

CREDITS

The Publisher would like to thank the following people for their valuable assistance with the preparation of this book:
British Airways History & Heritage: Paul Jarvis (britishairways.com/en-gb/information/about-ba/history-and-heritage)
Musée Air + Espace: Sylvie Lallement (museeairespace.fr)
RAF Museum: Peter Elliot (rafmuseum.org.uk)
Smithsonian National Air and Space Museum: Kate Igoe (airandspace.si.edu)
Fédération Aéronautique Internationale: Max Bishop (fia.org)
Musée du Fort de la Pompelle á Reims: Marc Bouxin and Valérie Chopin (reims.fr/culture-patrimoine/musees-et-collections-permanentes/fort-pompelle.htm)
Service Historique de la Défense, Chateau de Vincennes: Bertrand Fonck (servicehistorique.sga.defense.gouv.fr/Le-SHD-a-Vincennes.html)

PICTURE CREDITS

The publishers would like to thank the following sources for their kind permission to reproduce the pictures in this book.

Key: t = top, b = bottom, l = left, r = right and c = centre.

AKG-Images: 41b, 42bc, 45b, 68bl, 79;/ The Art Archive: 22t; /British Airways Archive and Museum Collection: 56, 57br, 60, 61, 71br, 73t, 73b, 112-113, 134bl, 136-137; /Corbis: 16bl, 32-33, 48-49, 49tr, 52-53, 62, 70-71, 87br, 62-63; /Bettmann: 2-3, 16br, 26r, 35-36, 37-38, 43, 51, 59b, 72r, 87t, 88t, 88-89, 96, 102-103, 106-107, 115 120-121, 122, 123t, 124-125, 126, 131br; /DPA: 151; /George Hall: 138, 140-141; /Jeremy Horner: 137t / Hulton-Deutsch Collection: 109, 129; /Museum of Flight: 6-7, 74bl; /Canada Aviation & Space Museum: 20l, 31; / Michael Nicholson: 20r; /David Pollack: 72l; /Reuters: 140, 143; /Reuters/Tech. Sgt. Howard Blair-USAF: 142-143; / Reuters/Kimimasa Mayama: 154; /H. Armstrong Roberts/ ClassicStock: 58; /Bill Ross: 142-143; /Rykoff Collection: 111t; /Skyscan: 144-145; /Sygma/Richard Melloul: 107br; / Transtock: 140t; /Underwood & Underwood: 10-11, 64bl; / Courtesy of Defence Visual Information Center: 117; / Fédération Aéronautique Internationale World Record Archives, Lausanne: 66, 67t; /Getty Images: 1, 9, 21t, 22t, 28-29, 32l, 34, 35, 36l, 39r, 46, 47t, 47b, 49br, 50, 57tl, 57tr, 65cl, 69tr; 75r, 77tr, 78t, 78b, 81t, 82-83, 84t, 87r, 88c, 92, 105, 107br, 118-119, 132, 133, 134-135,138-139, 141; /AFP: 154tl, 154b; /Spencer Platt: 155b; /Popperfoto: 39tr, 42c, 60l, 80b, 94-95, 111br; / Popperfoto/Bob Thomas: 29r; /Roger Viollet: 59tr; /Time & Life Pictures: 24, 68-69, 114, 123b; /Time & Life Pictures/ Charles Fenno Jacobs: 74tl; /Imperial War Museums: 4-5 (CH 740), 45 (Q 65535), 80t (HU 1062), 81b (CH 740), 84b (H 4219), 86l (CH 18005), 93br (CL 552); /Department of Documents: 85; /JSC History Collection, University of Houston/Clear Lake: 130, 131; /© KLM: 110; /Mary Evans: 26l; /Mirrorpix: 25t, 27, 28t, 104; /Musée de l'air et de l'espace: 24, 25b; /Musée du fort de a Pompelle a Reims: 41t; /NASA: 127, 128-129, 131tr; /National Archives and Records Administration, Washington: 14, 14-15, 97t, 97b, 98-99, 100, 101; /National Museum of the U.S. Air Force: 123l; /RAF Museum:;54-55, 65r /Rex Features: Action Press: 150; /Neale Hayes: 152-153; /Science & Society: Science Museum: 30, 108; /Service Historique de la Défence. Chateau de Vincennes: 40; /Shutterstock: 3; /Smithsonian Institution: 16t, 67b; /Topfoto.co.uk: 43t, 53br, 90-91, 93tr, 116-117; /Fotomos: 8b; /AP: 140b; /The Granger Collection: 10t, 12, 18r; /Roger-Viollet: 90l, 116-117; / Ullstein Bild: 76, 77

Every effort has been made to acknowledge correctly and contact the source and/or copyright holder of each picture, and Carlton Books apologizes for any unintentional errors or omissions, which will be corrected in future editions of this book.

MEMORABILIA CREDITS

Topfoto.co.uk/The Granger Collection page 13
RAF Museum page 54–5; page 65tr, br
Science Society/Science Museum page 30
Museé du fort de a Pompelle á Reims page 41t
British Airways Museum page 60–1; page 113; page 136 7b
Fédération Aéronautique Internationale World Record Archives, Lausanne page 66–7t
Smithsonian National Air and Space Museum page 25; 67b
The United States National Archives, Washington 100; 101
JSC History Collection, University of Houston/Clear Lake page 130–1l

Every effort has been made to acknowledge correctly and contact the source and/or copyright holder of each picture and piece of memorabilia, and Carlton Books apologizes for any unintentional errors or omissions, which will be corrected in future editions of this book.